JACQUES DE COUTRE'S
SINGAPORE
AND JOHOR
1594–c.1625

JACQUES DE COUTRE'S
SINGAPORE AND JOHOR
1594–c.1625

EDITED, ANNOTATED AND INTRODUCED
BY
PETER BORSCHBERG

NUS PRESS
SINGAPORE

Published with support from

郭仁伯

© Peter Borschberg

Published by:

NUS Press
National University of Singapore
AS3-01-02, 3 Arts Link
Singapore 117569

Fax: (65) 6774-0652
E-mail: nusbooks@nus.edu.sg
Website: http://nuspress.nus.edu.sg

ISBN 978-9971-69-852-2 (Paper)

First edition 2015
Reprint 2016

National Library Board Singapore Cataloguing in Publication Data

Coutre, Jacques de, 1577–1640, author.
 Jacques de Coutre's Singapore and Johor, 1594–c.1625 / [Jacques de Coutre];
 edited, annotated and introduced by Peter Borschberg. – Singapore: NUS Press,
 [2015]
  pages cm
  Includes bibliographic references.
  ISBN : 978-9971-69-852-2 (paperback)

 1. Coutre, Jacques de, 1577–1640 – Travel – Southeast Asia. 2. Southeast Asia -
Description and travel – Early works to 1800. 3. Singapore – History – 16th century.
4. Johor (Malaysia) – History – 16th century. 5. Southeast Asia – History – 16th
century. I. Title. II. Borschberg, Peter, editor.

DS522.2
959 -- dc23   OCN895097140

Cover image: Charles Dyce, Batu Blair or Sail Rock Old Straits of Singapore, 1846.
Watercolour and ink on paper (Source: National University of Singapore Museum
Collection, S1970-0052-047-0).

Designer: Nelani Jinadasa
Printed by: Mainland Press Pte Ltd

Contents

MEMORIALS

List of Abbreviations

BOC   Pieter van Dam, *Beschryvinge van de Oostindische Compagnie*, ed. by F.W. Stapel, 8 vols. (The Hague: Martinus Nijhoff, 1931–43).

CMJ   Peter Borschberg, ed., *Journal, Memorials and Letters of Cornelis Matelieff de Jonge: Security, Diplomacy and Commerce in 17th-century Southeast Asia* (Singapore: NUS Press, 2015).

EFS   Anthony Farrington and Dhiravat na Pombejra, ed., *The English Factory in Siam, 1612–1685*, 2 vols. (London: The British Library, 2007).

GLA   Mons. Sebastião Rodolfo Dalgado, *Glossário Luso-Asiático*, 2 vols. (Coimbra: Imprensa da Universidade, 1919–21).

GPFT   Peter Borschberg, *Hugo Grotius, the Portuguese and Free Trade in the East Indies* (Singapore and Leiden: NUS Press and KITLV Press, 2011).

GVOC   *VOC Glossarium. Verklaringen van Termen, verzamelt uit de Rijksgeschiedkundige Publicatiën die betrekking hebben op de Verenigde Oost-Indische Compagnie* (The Hague: Instituut voor Nederlandse Geschiedenis, 2000).

HJ   Henry Yule and A.C. Burnell, *Hobson-Jobson: A Glossary of Colloquial Anglo-Indian Words and Phrases*, reprint (Sittingbourne: Linguasia, 1994).

JDC	Peter Borschberg, ed., *The Memoirs and Memorials of Jacques de Coutre: Security, Trade and Society in 16th- and 17th-century Southeast Asia* (Singapore: NUS Press, 2014).
JMBRAS	Journal of the Malaysian Branch of the Royal Asiatic Society
JO	J.K.J. de Jonge, *Opkomst van het Nederlandsch gezag in Oost-Indië. Verzameling van onuitgegeven stukken uit het oud-coloniaal archief,* 16 vols. (The Hague: Martinus Nijhoff, 1862–1925).
JSEAS	Journal of Southeast Asian Studies
PSM	Paulo Jorge de Sousa Pinto, *The Portuguese and the Straits of Melaka, 1575–1619: Power, Trade and Diplomacy* (Singapore: NUS Press, 2012).
SMS	Peter Borschberg, *The Singapore and Melaka Straits: Violence, Security and Diplomacy in the 17th Century* (Singapore and Leiden: NUS Press and KITLV Press, 2010).
VOC	Vereenigde Oost-Indische Compagnie; United Netherlands East India Company; the Dutch East India Company

List of Illustrations

Acknowledgements

Research for this booklet was facilitated through a grant awarded by the Singapore Ministry of Education and the Faculty of Arts and Social Sciences of the National University of Singapore (R110-000-052-12), research funds from the National Archives, as well as the Lee Foundation, Singapore. A special word of gratitude is extended to the Toyo Bunko (the Oriental Library) in Tokyo, Japan, as well as to the international research and graduate training project "Baltic Borderlands" (IRTG 1540), based at the University of Greifswald and funded by the German Research Foundation (Deutsche Forschungsgemeinschaft, DFG).

This publication was supported by a generous donation by the heirs of the late Kuet Gin Bok.

Preface

This publication offers a selection of passages excerpted from *The Memoirs and Memorials of Jacques de Coutre: Security, Trade and Society in 16th- and 17th-century Southeast Asia* (2014). Its targeted readership is students, teachers and researchers interested in the history of Singapore, Johor and the Straits region before 1800. The introduction has been adapted from a public paper presented on the occasion of the book launch held at the Asian Civilisations Museum in Singapore on 29 January 2014.

The texts selected for translation and included in this volume are part of a bundle of manuscripts that contain De Coutre's autobiography and several memorials. This bound bundle is preserved at the National Library of Spain in Madrid.[1] Chapters from the *Vida* or autobiography of De Coutre have been excerpted and translated from book I, which covers Jacques's life in Southeast Asia between 1593 and 1603. No passages have been taken from the remaining two books that cover his life in Goa, his two return voyages to Europe and his subsequent deportation in 1623.

The glossary and list of place names has been reworked to fit the format and objective of this booklet. They offer information about functionaries, commodities and places mentioned in the main text that are not readily available in English or easy to source via reference works and the internet.

[1.] Madrid, National Library of Spain, Ms. 2780. See also Borschberg, "Jacques de Coutre as a Source for the Early 17th Century History of Singapore, the Johor River, and the Straits", *JMBRAS* 81, 2 (2008): 71–97, esp. 75–6.

Introduction

Who was Jacques de Coutre and why should we read him? Of what value are his writings to researchers of Singapore, the Peninsula and Southeast Asia at large?

The fact is that there are few written sources both Asian and European from which we can reconstruct the history of Singapore before 1800. Most of what was available detailed the sights mariners caught while passing through one of the three Singapore Straits: between present-day Sentosa and Harbourfront (Old Strait of Singapore), around the south-western side of present-day Sentosa, or further South through the main fairway used by international container shipping today. Eyewitness accounts of the people living around Singapore's islands were sparse, and direct references to the settlement or the port fewer still.

De Coutre's writings on Singapore are the single most substantive early modern source known to have survived. His first-hand testimonies of the Straits, of Singapore Island, and its settlement and port were written around 1625–29; they were unknown until the 1960s, and unpublished until the late 1980s. His insight into the region is astute: his recommendations to the Spanish and Portuguese crowns staked out a vision not dissimilar to the one later pursued by Sir Thomas Stamford Raffles in the early 19th century. This introduction looks at the life and writings of Jacques de Coutre and examines specifically what he had to say about Singapore, the Johor River and the upstream Johor royal residence at Batu Sawar.

Jacques Who?

We must first address one important question: Who was Jacques de Coutre?[1] Jacques de Coutre was born in the city of Bruges in Flanders around the year 1572.[2] According to his autobiography, or *Vida*, his father had passed away when he was young. In the second half of the 16th century, the Low Countries, including Flanders, were embroiled in the armed conflict that eventually became known as the Dutch Revolt. To escape the ravages of war, Jacques first tried his hand fishing for cod in the North Sea and subsequently made his way to Lisbon where he met up with his older brother Joseph. Here in Lisbon the two young men decided that they would try their luck in the East Indies.

The outbound voyage to Goa in 1592–93 was harrowing. Arriving in India, Joseph was so sick that he was unable to alight from the vessel.[3] Joseph later recuperated, married and settled in Goa. Curiosity, we are told, induced Jacques to embark alone on the next leg of his journey from Goa to Melaka, arriving on September 1593.[4] Melaka, as well as Manila, Patani and Johor's capital Batu Sawar, would serve as Jacques's base for the next eight years. In 1603 Jacques returned to Goa to marry Catarina do Couto.[5] Goa would serve as Jacques's new home for the next two decades. According to his autobiography, he undertook voyages to Europe, proceeding overland through the Persian Gulf, Basra and Aleppo to the Mediterranean and on to Spain. In 1623 Jacques and

---

[1.] Concerning earlier studies on Jacques de Coutre and his works, see esp. *Aziatische Omzwervingen. Het levensverhaal van Jaques de Coutre, een Brugs diamantenhandelaar, 1591–1626*, tr. Johan Verbeckmoes and Eddy Stols (Berchem: EPO, 1988); J. de Coutre, *Como Remediar o Estado da Índia? Being the Appendices of the Vida de Jaques de Coutre* (Madrid: Biblioteca Nacional, Ms. 2780), ed. Benjamin N. Teesma (Leiden: Centre for the History of European Expansion, 1989); and Jacques de Coutre, *Andanzas asiáticas*, ed. Eddy Stols, Benjamin Teensma and Johan Verbeckmoes (Madrid: História 16, 1991).

[2.] This is earlier than has been hitherto believed. See Borschberg, ed., *The Memoirs and Memorials of Jacques de Coutre: Security, Trade and Society in 16th- and 17th-century Southeast Asia* (Singapore: NUS Press, 2014), pp. xxvii and 2.

[3.] JDC, pp. 36, 72.

[4.] JDC, pp. 18, 38–9, 73–4.

[5.] JDC, pp. 11, 35, 49.

Joseph were arrested for breaching immigration laws and colluding with the Dutch. They were subsequently deported from Goa to Lisbon.[6] There, under pressure from the powerful resident Flemish merchant community, officials released and transferred the brothers to Madrid on the grounds that, as citizens of Bruges and also of Flanders, Jacques and Joseph were also subjects of the King of Spain and Portugal, Philip IV/III.[7]

This period—the late 1620s and early 1630s—was when Jacques wrote a series of memorials and petitions to the crowns of Spain and Portugal, and evidently also his autobiography, *Vida de Jaques de Couttre* (Life of Jacques de Coutre). Ostensibly penned as a means of exonerating himself and his brother and also ingratiating himself with Iberian crown officials, the memorials provide a sweeping overview of trading networks in the East Indies. They also stake out security priorities aimed at stemming the perceived decline and institutional decay of Portuguese India. The *Vida* is preserved in neat copy and, judging by the draft title page featured at the beginning of the manuscript, was aimed at publication.[8] In a move to brandish his Portuguese credentials, Jacques sometimes assumed his wife's family name, signing off as "Jaques do Couto" on a series of briefs and memoranda.[9]

In 1632, Jacques and Joseph were finally exonerated by the Council of Portugal.[10] It does not appear that they ever returned to India, nor would it appear that the goods confiscated at the time of their deportation from Goa were ever restored to them. Jacques passed away in the city of Saragossa in 1640. He was buried in the hospital San Andrés in Madrid, which is said to have served chiefly members of the Flemish community in the Spanish capital city and no longer stands.[11]

6. JDC, pp. xxviii, 15–6, 20–1.
7. JDC, p. 21.
8. An image of this draft title page is reproduced in JDC on p. 22.
9. JDC, pp. 1–2, 200n27.
10. JDC, pp. xxviii, 21, 23, 32.
11. JDC, pp. xxviii, 22.

The Manuscripts

The second question we must ask is: What do we know about the pedigree of these texts? Do they have a specific agenda or objective, and if so, what might these be? Research conducted on the memorials of Jacques de Coutre over the past four decades has yielded some important insights. First, the writings were all almost certainly written for the express purpose of facilitating his exoneration by the Council of Portugal. Second, Jacques was only one in a prolific family of *arbitristas* (project writers) who, according to Juan José Morales, provided "economic analysis of a particular problem with a 'project' or recommendation for recovery. These were mainly pragmatic, but could also be foolish."[12] In view of the dramatic shifts in the roles played by the Western powers in Asia, the objective of these *arbitristas* was to counter both the erosion of the *Estado da Índia*'s power as well as the decay of Portuguese commercial networks across the Indian Ocean region. The memorials are written in a hand that is not easy to read and the texts themselves are fairly straightforward, unadorned and business-like, if on occasion also repetitive.

The *Vida* could not offer a sharper contrast. It is a "fast-paced" text, "full of colour", packed with action, exotic curiosities, torture and cruelty, as well as whimsical Asian despots.[13] In his review of De Coutre published in *The Star* (Kuala Lumpur), Colin Goh claimed it read like a "swash-buckling Hollywood tale" … written by an author who was a "very good raconteur with an eye for detail on matters he experienced."[14] It is clear that, as he imagined a text destined for wider circulation and readership, De Coutre was pandering to his prospective readers' tastes and prejudices. One question lingers: who was responsible for infusing the *Vida* with elements of the

---

[12]   J.J. Morales, review of "The Memoirs and Memorials of Jacques de Coutre", *Asian Review of Books,* 26 January 2014, http://www.asianreviewofbooks.com/new/?ID=1732.

[13]   Zakir Hussain, "Rare look into South-East Asia from 400 Years Ago. Trader's Account Details its Political Trading Landscape", *The Straits Times,* 18 January 2014, D17.

[14]   Colin Goh, "Tales from the East. The Memoirs and Memorials of Jacques de Coutre", *The Star* (Kuala Lumpur), 10 June 2014, p. 15.

picturesque and Byzantine novels—both very popular genres of literature during the golden age of 17th-century Spain?[15] As we know from the draft title page of the *Vida*, Jacques's son Esteban is known to have exercised some role as editor in shaping the text for publication.[16] So another question naturally arises: does this shaping of the *Vida* to popular literary preferences of the day actually diminish its value as a primary source and information trove? In the end, is Jacques de Coutre just another Marco Polo or Fernão Mendes Pinto who are known to have interwoven their accounts with second or third-hand stories and hearsay, and claimed these to be their own?[17] Can we—and should we—trust him? Or should we simply discount his narrative as fiction?

Let us first separate the notions of content and form. How useful are early modern travel materials as repositories of long-lost knowledge? How careful should one be when evaluating and citing such texts? In terms of content, what differentiates Marco Polo and Mendes Pinto from De Coutre is authenticity and factual accuracy; the former have come to be seen as "liars", their writings replete with both information and disinformation because they retell stories second or even third hand. We cannot say the same for De Coutre, whose account is generally accurate, with interesting and delightful details. In terms of form, it must be said that the autobiographical element does not turn nonfiction into fiction. Even today, autobiographies follow predictable tropes of rags-to-riches or an underdog overcoming major obstacles to achieve success. Nobody wants to read about the easy life of a person born into a privileged and nurturing family.

---

15. This question was raised and discussed by G.D. Winius and Carrie C. Chorba, "Literary Invasions in *La vida de Jaques de Coutre*: do they prejudice its value as an historical source?" in *A Carreira da Índia e as Rotas dos Estreitos. Actas do VIII Seminário Internacional de História Indo-Portuguesa,* ed. Artur Teodoro de Matos and Luís Filipe R. Thomaz (Angra do Heroísmo: Barbosa & Javier, 1998), pp. 709–19. See also Borschberg, "Jacques de Coutre as a Source", pp. 71–97.

16. JDC, pp. 1, 23, 30; Borschberg, "Jacques de Coutre as a Source", pp. 77–8; Winius and Chorba, "Literary Invasions", p. 712.

17. JDC, pp. xxviii, 29; Borschberg, "Jacques de Coutre as a Source", pp. 79–80.

In conclusion, Jacques—or his son Esteban—may very well have streamlined the information according to contemporary tastes and projected readership, but there is not a shade of doubt that we have here a valuable eyewitness report, even if this report was recorded well after the actual events.[18] The factual accuracy and autobiography is replete with interesting information, and the *Vida* is a text still capable of capturing the imagination of most readers today.

Scholars and historians are probably more interested in the insights presented in the memorials. A different set of challenges and questions emerge with the memorials but the crucial difference is that the memorials were written to inform and prompt action, not to delight or entertain as the case with the *Vida*. The memorials are neither written in any particular literary style nor do they indulge in painting images of exotic curiosities and tyrannical Asian rulers. As Juan José Morales has very aptly highlighted in his lengthy assessment of *The Memoirs and Memorials* published in the *Asian Review of Books*, "some of the most interesting insights are [De Coutre's] strong advocacy of free trade and free enterprise." Morales perceptively explained:

> De Coutre criticizes the old forms of patronage—in particular the concession system, common to Spain and Portugal for so long, whereby the Crown authorizes and then shares profits or imposes a tax in the venture—for being unreliable, inefficient and unpredictable. Instead, he proposes easing restrictions to trade, lowering duties and leaving commerce in the hands of private merchants who would undercut the Dutch by virtue of the mechanism of competition.[19]

In other words, Jacques was something of an economic visionary, a facet of his intelligence that did not escape the keen attention of León Gómez Rivas of the Instituto Juan de Mariana in Madrid; he

---

18. See Chris Baker, review of "The Memoirs and Memorials of Jacques de Coutre", *Journal of the Siam Society* 102, 1 (2014): 294–6, esp. p. 295.
19. J.J. Morales, review of "The Memoirs and Memorials of Jacques de Coutre".

wondered aloud if De Coutre was familiar with the writings of the authors of the so-called School of Salamanca of the 16th and 17th centuries.[20]

Given the dense style in which they are written, the memorials admittedly do not make for easy reading, which can easily interfere with an objective evaluation of their merits. It sometimes appears that De Coutre's frustrations with the Portuguese clouded his assessment of the broader issues at hand, and in any case the memorials show a distinct propensity to pour scorn over the Portuguese, and in turn, praise the Spanish (specifically the Castilians) for their accomplishments in Asia and beyond. Despite their anti-Lusitanian tone, the memorials impart important information about networks, trade, business opportunities, goods and commodities, as well as the state of the Dutch and English competition, and offer valuable insights to researchers engaged in different branches of scholarly inquiry, ranging from history through anthropology. The ostensible purpose of De Coutre's memorials is to highlight to the Spanish Crown and the Portuguese viceroy in Goa what the Portuguese have lost to the Dutch and English competitors. He makes a series of recommendations that he thinks will be able to stem— if not reverse—the declining fortunes of Portuguese Asia.[21] The information about trade and trading networks provided in the memorials—as well as to a more limited extent in the *Vida*—enable us to reconstruct and identify the complex system of trade and exchange of precious stones, commodities, spices and medicinal produce from Southeast Asia with finished goods, especially textiles, from the Indian subcontinent, predominantly from the Coromandel Coast, Gujarat, as well as Bengal.[22] There is hardly a

---

[20]. L. Gómez Rivas, "Quinientos años del descubrimiento del Pacífico", 29 January 2014, http://www.juandemariana.org/comentario/6474/quinientos/anos/descubrimiento/pacifico.

[21]. JDC, pp. 34, 54.

[22]. This is a point also made by Patricia Bjaaland in her review of the *Memoirs and Memorials of Jacques de Coutre* posted 30 January 2014. See http://www.goodreads.com/review/show/833834229: "I wish this work had been available a few years ago when I was doing some research on Indian trade textiles as it would have filled in some gaps in where some of those remarkable textiles were sent.... The

set of period documents that provide such a plethora of information on commodities, networks and exchange in such an explicit and detailed manner. Nor are there many period documents dating from the 16th and early 17th centuries that yield such a comprehensive overview of trade in the Indian Ocean region, ranging from the eastern coast of Africa to the Japanese islands.

De Coutre's account of Siam during the reign of King Naresuan (Phra Naret, Samphet II), while admittedly problematic in many ways, is nevertheless one of the oldest—if not the oldest—European eyewitness account of the former Siamese capital city, and the only known eyewitness account of the great King Naresuan. Jacques's Siamese adventure, which took place around 1595 and 1596 together with his later visit to Patani[23] toward the end of 1602, merits in itself an in-depth discussion elsewhere. While the scholarly excitement surrounding the Siam chapters of the *Vida* is certainly warranted, I want to highlight the value of these sources for the history of the southern Malay Peninsula. In addition to offering the oldest substantive European eyewitness account of Ayutthaya, Jacques also furnishes what is beyond doubt the most comprehensive account of Singapore, including its adjacent islands and straits that survive in any language dating before 1800.

Two locations have been selected to showcase the ways in which the writings of De Coutre can also be useful to historians of the Malay Peninsula, including also of Portuguese Melaka.

Singapore

What does De Coutre have to say about Singapore? Some readers might find this question bewildering: Was there even *anything* in Singapore worth mentioning at the turn of the 16th and early 17th centuries? What, and how much, could he possibly write about? Surprisingly, a lot. So much, in fact, that in the preface to the 2014

Index contains half a page of entries that reads: 'take to Aceh; take to Arabia; from Cambay; to Cambodia; to Champa; to Mombasa, to Mozambique, from Sindh....' "

[23.]   See the list of place names (*Patani*).

edition, I noted that his observations on Singapore collectively form the bulk of information we have about the island from the period before 1800.[24]

Jacques's observations and statements about Singapore can be divided into three categories. The first we can term incidental or casual statements that touch on the maritime spaces located to the south of Singapore Island, relating mainly to the Old and New Straits of Singapore; the second concerns the island Jacques referred to as *Isla de Arena* or present-day Sentosa; and the third is a memorial that carefully examines security issues for Singapore, the straits, and the upstream towns of the Johor River region. In this document De Coutre proposed the construction of three fortifications on what would now be sovereign territory of Singapore, namely: on Sentosa, around Changi Point, and a third small one off Pulau Tekong Besar,[25] the latter meant "to patrol the entire [Johor] River and to prevent both large and small *junks*[26] from entering." To this end Jacques advanced a plan for a set of fortifications that, with hindsight, is nothing less than prophetic. He advised:[27]

[Your Majesty] should become the lord of this port [i.e., *Sabandaría*, Singapore], which is one of the best that serves the [East] Indies. [Your Majesty] can build a city there and become lord of this kingdom.

Let us now dissect the statements about Singapore in a bit more detail, starting with the aforementioned exhortation to acquire sovereignty over Singapore Island and found a colonial trading emporium on it. But before that, we need to bear three points in mind:

First, Jacques drafted his proposals about *two full centuries* before Sir Thomas Stamford Raffles arrived in 1819 and founded the British trading post on Singapore.

24. JDC, p. xxi.
25. JDC, p. 235; Borschberg, "Jacques de Coutre as a Source", pp. 87–8.
26. A type of sailing ship of various sizes, generally featured a double (wooden) hull, one or several masts, and sails made of cloth or woven reeds. See JDC, p. 325.
27. JDC, pp. 234–5 and below, p. 82.

Second, we must cast entrenched habits aside in thinking that pre-Raffles Singapore was an abandoned, unseen and unrecognised place forgotten by time. As Zakir Hussain so aptly put it in his review of *The Memoirs and Memorials* published in *The Straits Times* of 18 January 2014, "It is de Coutre's descriptions of Singapore in that period that are the most detailed and strengthen the case that it was already a hub for shipping more than 200 years before the British arrived."[28]

Third, if Jacques was capable of devising concrete and specific plans for the acquisition of sovereignty over Singapore Island, and proposing the founding of a colonial trading emporium, then we must invariably concede that such a vision could not have been the unique brainchild of a genius named Raffles. This has very serious consequences for our understanding of Singapore's history over the *longue durée,* for it calls into question the long-held view that Raffles was a specially gifted person with a unique vision for Singapore Island. Sure, both men had a common vision. The difference is that De Coutre had a clear vision and plan and relied on someone else to execute them, while Raffles went ahead and took steps to execute them himself.

Let us return to the discussion of what insight we can gain from De Coutre's observations about Singapore. Firstly, why did he advise the king of Spain to acquire sovereignty over Singapore and found a colonial emporium there?[29]

> [Your Majesty] should become the lord of this port which is
> one of the best that serves the [East] Indies.

This is a very powerful statement. Not only is Jacques firstly acknowledging that Singapore had a viable and functioning port, he states that it is the "best". What does that mean here? Since it was certainly not the biggest or the busiest port, we should most probably understand the word "best" as a statement about Singapore's location. We may even want to stretch this bit and

---

[28.] Zakir Hussain, "Rare Look", *The Straits Times*, 18 January 2014, D.17.

[29.] JDC, pp. 234–5 and below, p. 82.

claim that it refers to Singapore's unique and convenient location along the main shipping arteries of the day. This is a crucial insight about Singapore's strategic position and geographic setting. Further evidence of the existence of a harbour was that Singapore had a settlement De Coutre named *Sabandaria*, no doubt named after the presence of a *shahbandar* or harbourmaster on the island.[30] One only has a harbourmaster if there is actually a harbour or a port. In fact, the island as a whole he named *Isla de la Sabandaria Vieja*, "Island of the Old Sabandaria" or liberally "of the shahbandar's compound". It all fits.

What else does he say? Let us take a closer look at the next sentence:[31]

> We anchored in front of a place which is called *Sabandaría*, which is inhabited by Malays, subjects of the king of Johor to whom the *saletes*, who sail in the straits, pay tribute.

This means that Jacques was aboard a vessel that had anchored just off a settlement he calls *Sabandaria*, which would have presumably been just adjacent to that port or harbour that he claimed was "the best that served the East Indies". Let us now turn to see what Jacques has to say about the *saletes*, a collective term for different tribes of the sea, the *orang laut*.[32] Referring to a trip by sea he had undertaken to the port of Pahang[33] in 1594, De Coutre recalled the following at the western entrance to the Old Strait of Singapore:[34]

[30.] The presence of a *shahbandar* on Singapore about a decade later (1606) is confirmed in the travelogue of VOC Admiral Cornelis Matelieff de Jonge. See CMJ, document I, p. 64. See also the glossary (*shahbandar*).

[31.] JDC, p. 79 and below, p. 47.

[32.] See the glossary (*orang laut*).

[33.] See the list of place names (*Pahang*).

[34.] JDC, pp. 77–8 and below, pp. 46–7; Zakir Hussein, "Rare Look", *The Straits Times*, 18 January 2014, D.17; also Borschberg, "Jacques de Coutre as a Source", p. 85. This testimony of De Coutre is strikingly similar to the one recorded somewhat later in 1637. See Richard Carnac Temple, ed., *The Travels of Peter Mundy in Europe and Asia, 1608–1667*, III, Travels in England, India, China, etc. (London: Hakluyt Society, 1919), p. 146, entry for 1 June 1637, "The First of this Month wee wentt through the old straightt which May bee aboutt a

Many fishermen live along these straits, who are called *saletes*. While pointing out the strait to us, they came aboard our ship with fresh fish and a lot of local fruits, which are very different from the fruits in Europe, and which they pick in the hills. Some are called durians, and others are called mangosteens, and others are called *rambai* and *buah duku*;[35] they are all very healthy and tasty. They brought us many parasols made from palm leafs—they call them *payones*[36]—and fresh water. They gave us everything in exchange for rice and old fabrics. They are extremely poor people. They live in some sloops[37] that are at most five or six *varas*[38] long, and are very narrow, made of thin, light planks, and on them they have their houses with wives and children, dogs, cats, and even hens with their chicks. They raise everything inside the little sloop, which amazed me because these boats are so narrow. When they go fishing, the man sits on the *perahu*[39] with a harpoon and the wife and children paddle very fast and very skilfully. Very old men can be found among them; who said that all of them were a hundred years old. They are treacherous people by nature. For this reason we deal with them very carefully and with weapons in our hands, because it has happened that they were allowed to come aboard our ships in such numbers, ostensibly

---

good league in length and not above ¼ Mile broade att the Coming in and going outt, butt within wider, with many little baies, Creeks, Ilands, etts., Where wee saw sundry companies of small boates covered over with Mattes, which is the Ordinary habitation of those thatt live among these Ilands, Where they have their wives, children and Household goods."

[35]. This fruit is variously also known as *langsat* (with different orthography) in different parts of Southeast Asia. The Hokkien name is *bah luku*.

[36]. This is a corruption of the Malay word *payung*; a parasol.

[37]. A single-masted sailing boat featuring a lateen (triangular) mainsail and a headsail. De Coutre also uses the term to describe the vessel of the *orang laut*.

[38]. An Iberian measurement of length, ranging from 83 centimetres to 1.1 metres. See JDC, p. 347.

[39]. A type of small craft that can be either sailed or rowed. The term is very elastic in its application, and vessel types covered by this category range from coastal cargo ships (that are chiefly sailed) to longboats on a river. See JDC, pp. 334–5; SMS, p. 334.

to sell fresh fish, and in the blink of an eye they attacked and killed everyone aboard the ship. They are armed with poisoned daggers, which they call *kerisses*,[40] and spears made of wild palm, without any iron. They are called *seligis*[41] and they throw them so hard that they can even penetrate an iron breastplate and any shield no matter how sturdy they are.

Here we have what is almost certainly the oldest and fairly detailed European eyewitness account of the *orang laut* living in the waters around Singapore during the precolonial age. The passage is particularly interesting for three reasons. First, unlike the imperialists later in the 19th century, De Coutre did not portray the *orang laut* in an entirely negative light, and he never alluded to them as "pirates" in this passage. For sure, they are poor and unpredictable as later European accounts would attest to, but Jacques also emphasised that the *saletes* were entrepreneurial in an honest way. They sold or bartered fish and fruit to passing ships.

Second, De Coutre expressed some admiration for the *saletes*, wondering aloud how it is that they were comfortable living with their children, animals and small livestock in very limited space. He also expressed admiration at the old age some of them had evidently reached. He regarded them chiefly as guides and flying vendors (admittedly with a propensity to violence) and, as said, never called them "pirates".

Third, the martial skills of the *selates* or *orang laut* are of course well known, but here we have a description of their two main weapons: the keris and the *seligi*, spears made of the wild palm and without using any metal. But the tips of those spears are just as good as having been made of iron, for they can penetrate a metal breast plate or even a shield.[42]

---

40. A Malay (ceremonial) dagger. See JDC, p. 326.
41. A type of short spear that is made without any metal. See also the glossary (*seligi*).
42. JDC, p. 79.

Jaques de coutre

lupas q̃ tienen de largo cinco o seis varas;
quando mucho, y muy angostas hechas de
tablas ligeras, y delgadas, y alli tienen su
caza con mugeres y hijos, perros gatos hasta
galinas con sus pollos, crian alli todo den-
tro de la chalupilla q̃ me admire de uer
por la estrecheza.

Pues quando uan pescando el hombre
se pone en la proa con un arpon, y la mu-
ger y los hijos reman con mucha uelozidad
y destroza y entre ellos ay hombres muy vie-
jos yo he conocido algunos que dezian te-
ner cada qual cien años de edad, y es gente
de su natural traydora, por ese respecto tra-
tamos con ellos com mucho cuidado, y con armas en las manos, por q̃ ha succedido dexar-
los entrar en nuebros nauios en tanta quan-
tidad al descuido como que uenian auen-
der pescado, alcabo y matar a todos los del
nauio, traen por armas unas dagas de pon-
çoña, q̃ ellos llaman crizes; y dardos sin
hierro hechos de palma braua, los llaman
saligas, y tiran tan rezio q̃ passan un pe:
to

Text page from the *Vida de Jaques de Coutre* (autobiography), book 1, chapter 3, describing how *saletes* or *selates* (*orang laut*) fish in the Straits of Singapore. (Madrid, National Library of Spain, Ms. 2780, fol. 11)

What De Coutre had to say about the *orang laut* living on their boats around Singapore Island is confirmed by a little-known Portuguese source preserved in the National Library of Portugal and titled "Explanation of the Maps and Description of all of the Fortresses, Cities and Towns which the Portuguese have in the Eastern Estado da Índia".[43] The manuscript dates from the first half of the 17th century and is thus contemporaneous with Jacques de Coutre. With reference to Singapore, it reads:[44]

> The Strait of Singapore has many channels and they are so narrow that in some parts the yardarms touch the trees; the water is so clear that fish can be seen in the depths and the sailors buy them from the locals, who are called Saletes, while [the fish] are still in the water; and they go with their wives and children in their boats to spear them in order to earn the promised price....

Barreto de Resende, another Portuguese-language author writing around this period (early 17th century), described the ports and the goods that could be traded along the littoral of the Singapore Straits in the aftermath of the Acehnese invasions of 1613 and 1615.[45] In this context, De Resende emphasised how much revenue Johor and Pahang made from trade, as he saw it, generated at the expense of Portuguese Melaka. What is striking about this passage is that no mention is made of a port or settlement on Singapore Island. Commercial activity and the population instead seem to have focused on the southern side of the Singapore Straits on the islands of Bulan and Bintan. De Resende's testimony confirms what

---

43. *Relação das Plantas & Descripções de todas as Fortalezas, Cidades & Povoações que os Portuguezes tem no Estado da India Oriental* (Lisbon: Biblioteca Nacional, 1936).
44. *Relação das Plantas*, pp. 45–6.
45. Aceh was a river, port and polity in northern Sumatra. It was especially important in the context of the pepper trade. Other commodities commonly sold in Aceh included nutmeg, mace and cloves, cotton pieces as well as opium. Concerning the Acehnese invasion of Johor in 1613, see SMS, pp. 112–5.

we know from archaeological evidence in Singapore.[46] While De Coutre could still describe the port and settlement at the time of his visit in 1594, their destruction about one and a half decades later by the Acehnese or other hostile forces would relegate the settlement to near oblivion. De Resende observed:[47]

> … [T]his city of Bintan was repopulated with many people and many fortifications for the love of Aceh. This king of Johor and Pahang [also] has other inhabited islands here [i.e. in this region] that are of minor significance. And in these regions next to the Singapore Strait is the port of Bullá [i.e., Bulan] which is densely populated by Malays [and] frequented by many merchants from across the whole South from where they come to sell their spices [and] from which the king of Pahang [and Johor] reaps considerable revenue.…

The excerpt evidences that the principal port around the straits was not the one located on Singapore Island, but across the straits and almost certainly on present-day Bulan. Its regional prominence is also confirmed in cartographical materials of Portuguese origin (where it is spelled in Portuguese as *Bullá* or *Buláo*), such as for example the hand-drawn chart of André Pereira dos Reis dating from around 1654. This particular specimen is preserved in the Dr. W.A. Engelbrecht Collection at the Maritiem Museum Rotterdam.[48]

[46.] John N. Miksic, *Singapore and the Silk Road of the Sea, 1300–1800* (Singapore: NUS Press, 2013). For earlier accounts of Singapore's archaeological finds, see esp. Miksic, *Archeological Research on the "Forbidden Hill" of Singapore: Excavations at Fort Canning, 1984* (Singapore: National Museum, 1985).

[47.] See Barreto de Resende, "Mallaqua. Descripsam da Fortalleza de Mallaqua" in *The Commentaries of the Great A. Dalboquerque, Second Viceroy of India*, Brás de Albuquerque, tr. Walter de Gray Birch, 4 vols. (London: Hakluyt Society, 1875–95), III, appendix I, pp. 273–4. Translated from the original Portuguese.

[48.] Rotterdam, Maritiem Museum, Collectie Dr. W.A. Engelbrecht, WAE 900–10. The entry reads: "entrada de [B]uláo" (entrance to Bulan [harbour] or port of Bulan)." This chart also features the names *Xabandaria* (*Shahbandaria* or *shahbandar's* compound) at an unnamed estuary (possibly the Singapore River or the nearby Kallang River estuary) and also the name Singapura (on the island). With reference to the latter, however, it remains insufficiently clear what the name Singapura exactly refers to.

Forts for Singapore

The period during which De Coutre lived in Melaka marked a crucial period of transition for the Portuguese in Asia. The close of the 16th and dawn of the 17th centuries saw the arrival of the first Dutch ships in the waters around the Malay Peninsula. Projecting their ongoing European conflict against the Iberian powers of Spain and Portugal into the Asian theatre, the Dutch quickly came to recognize the singular strategic importance of the waters around Singapore and regularly scoured these in search of richly-laden Portuguese merchant vessels arriving from ports further east, such as in China and Japan. What had begun as the seizure of a few vessels around the Malay Peninsula quickly emerged as a burning security issue for the Portuguese.[49] Threats to the security of Portuguese mercantile shipping, however, did not just emanate from the plundering activities of the Dutch East India Company (VOC). Expanding rapidly under the rule of Iskandar Muda in the first half of the 17th century, Aceh had attacked Johor in 1613 and then again in 1615, a traumatic event with far-reaching repercussions politically as well as economically. Jacques was certainly aware of these developments.

It is against the backdrop of such security concerns that we are to situate De Coutre's memorial, which proposed the construction of fortifications on the island of Singapore, as well as on nearby Sentosa. Before we turn to examine his plans in more detail it is useful to say a few words about how Jacques envisioned the waterways that are located to the south of the main island of Singapore.

---

[49]. Borschberg, "Portuguese, Spanish and Dutch plans to construct a Fort in the Straits of Singapore ca. 1584–1625", *Archipel* 65 (2003): 55–88; Borschberg, "From Self-Defence to an Instrument of War: Dutch Privateering Around the Malay Peninsula in the Early Seventeenth Century", *Journal of Early Modern History* 17 (2013): 35–52; Borschberg, "The Seizure of the *Sta. Catarina* Revisited: The Portuguese Empire in Asia, VOC Politics and the Origins of the Dutch-Johor Alliance (c. 1602–1616)", *JSEAS* 33, 1 (2002): 31–62; Borschberg, "A Portuguese-Dutch Naval Battle in the Johor River Estuary and the Liberation of Johor Lama in 1603", in *Early Singapore, 1300s–1819: Evidence in Maps, Text and Artefacts*, ed. J.N. Miksic and C-A.M.G. Low (Singapore: History Museum, 2004), pp. 106–17.

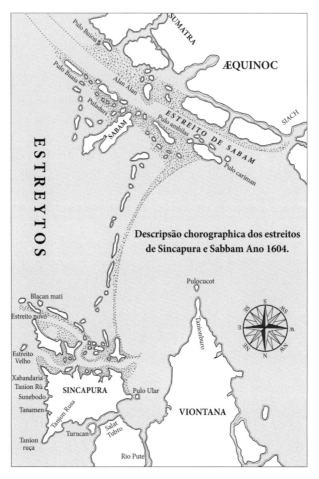

Redrawn map of Singapore and the adjacent straits by Manuel Godinho de Erédia and dated 1604. This map is found on fol. 61 of the original manuscript of his *Description of Melaka* believed to have been completed around 1613. The island of Singapore features several key toponyms on and around the island, including the entrances to the New and the Old Straits (*Estreito Novo* and *Estreito Velho*), *Xabandaria* (the settlement *Sabandaría*), *Tanion Rû* (Tanjong Rhu), *Sunebodo* (Sungei Bedok), *Tanamen* (Tanah Merah) as well as *Tanion Ruça* and *Tanion Rusa* (Tanjung Rusa, present-day Changi Point). *Turucan* or *Turuçan* is a phonetic corruption of the Malay word *terusan* (channel, canal, thoroughfare), and *Salat Tubro* is the Selat Teberau (Teberau Strait). Pulau Merambong at the western entrance to the Johor Strait is named *Pulo Ular* (Snake Island, sometimes also Ilha das Cobras).

The two main straits of Singapore located to the south of the main island were known from Portuguese and other European sources as the Old and the New Straits. The Old Strait of Singapore "is situated between one island and the other"—that is between the *Isla de la Sabandaría Vieja* and the *Isla de Arena,* or between modern Singapore Island and Sentosa. It is located around the present-day Harbourfront and Keppel Marina area and is said to feature strong, visible currents that give the appearance of a flowing river. It is a very narrow waterway which, as the memorial further explains, could be closed off by spanning a chain across, a measure designed to prevent larger ships from passing through. Further details of the Old Strait can also be found in De Coutre's *Vida.* Describing his voyage by sea to the city and kingdom of Pahang in 1594, he observed in book I, chapter III:[50]

> The following day we unfurled our sails and passed the islands Pulau Pisang[51] and Pulau Karimun [which are located] near the Strait of Singapore. [The area around Singapore] is completely covered with large and leafy trees, so much that when ships pass by, the tips of their yards inevitably brush along the branches, especially in the Old Strait of Singapore. The passage is very narrow and there is a great deal of [maritime] traffic with many ships from different kingdoms.

The Old Strait was sufficiently deep for ships of "three or four decks" to pass though, an observation that can be easily confirmed by consulting other sources describing the passage through the Old Strait in the 16th and 17th centuries.[52]

The New Strait of Singapore followed the south-western shores of present-day Sentosa. In some sources of the late 16th and early 17th centuries, especially the Portuguese chronicle of João de Barros, the New Strait was supposedly also known as the "Strait of

---

50. JDC, p. 75 and below, p. 46; Borschberg, "Jacques de Coutre as a Source", p. 84.
51. See the list of place names (*Pulau Pisang*).
52. JDC, p. 231.

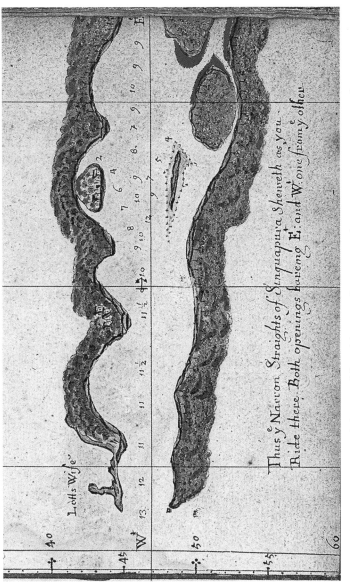

Section of an anonymous English map of the Old Strait of Singapore, the narrow maritime passage between present-day Sentosa (bottom) and the Keppel Harbour-Harbourfront region (top). The western entrance to the strait is marked by the stone formation Lot's Wife (alias Batu Berlayer, Longyamen, Varela). Also the triangular shape of Pulau Hantu (top centre) is clearly visible. (© The British Library Board, ADD. 15737, f10r)

Santa Barbara".[53] But this is admittedly the only source to provide this alternative name. De Coutre did not have much to say about the features of the New Strait, but was certainly clear about its strategic significance.

The north-western tip of Sentosa at present-day Fort Siloso is where the two maritime arteries, the Old and the New Straits of Singapore, converged. Jacques named this rocky point *Surgídera*.[54] The etymological root of this toponym is uncertain. On the one hand it could derive from the Portuguese *surgir*, which means "to rise". This could be a reference to the stone cliff rising from the waters that in the words of Jacques is a fortification by nature. It could also possibly be a derivative of the word *surgidoiro*, which means "anchorage". *Surgídera* was a point of anchorage described by Jacques where "carracks[55] remain here for seven or eight days without being able to sail through because of contrary winds, even when the tide is in their favour."[56]

Before examining Jacques's plans for the proposed fortification at *Surgídera* point, let us first take a closer look at what he had to say in general about the island he called *Isla de Arena*, present-day Sentosa. Mariners were almost certainly more familiar with this island than the main island of Singapore nearby, for it was evidently a well-known watering hole for passing ships. Jacques also described how he was sent to fetch fresh water there:[57]

> In the middle of the Singapore Straits [that is between the New and the Old Straits] there is an island, which measures more or less 3 leguas.[58] The Old Strait is situated on one side

---

53. João de Barros, Diogo do Couto, *Da Ásia. Dos feitos que os Portuguezes fizeram no conquista, e descubrimento das terras e mares do Oriente* (Lisbon: Na Regia Officina Typographia, 1778), XXI, pp. 210–1; also Carl Alexander Gibson-Hill, "Singapore Old Strait and New Harbour, 1300–1870", *Memoirs of the Raffles Museum*, no. 3 (Singapore: Government Printing Office, 1956), p. 52.

54. See JDC, pp. 381–2.

55. A large and generally lightly-armed Portuguese trading ship similar to a galleon. See also the glossary (*carrack*).

56. JDC, p. 233.

57. JDC, pp. 227, 229 and below, pp. 77–8.

58. A unit to measure distance; "mile". It is not quite certain which "*legua*"

of this island, the New Strait on the other. This island forms a rocky point which is located between the two Straits and that resembles a fortress created by nature. The point is called Surgídera; the Old Strait lies to one side of it, and the New Strait on the other.… [A]ll the vessels that pass through these straits … stop and drop anchor around the said point.

His adventure near the island in 1595 briefly reads:[59]

[I was asked] with three companions to fetch fresh water on an island that was called Isla de Arena. We approached it, I got the water. By the time we returned night had fallen. I could not see our junk, they did not light either a lamp nor did they fire any shots, even though I made many signals. [This lasted] until the current carried me out of the New Strait [of Singapore] and I saw them at anchor. At the entrance to this strait I came across some orang laut vessels, who attacked us in order to capture us, we repelled them however, by means of our barrel guns,[60] and one of my companions was injured. We rowed the entire night until we saw the junk at dawn and we managed to reach it feeling fed up and irritated.

The north-western tip of the island at the confluence of the Old and New Straits of Singapore called *Surgídera* Point was Jacques's preferred location for the first of two proposed fortifications on Singapore. He explained the situation to his monarch as follows:[61]

---

or "mile" De Coutre had in mind here. The unit named *legua* used to measure distances at sea was about six kilometres, whereas the corresponding unit for measuring distances overland was around two kilometres. The latter would appear closer to the geographic realities, in other words a distance of 6 rather than of 18 kilometres.

[59.] JDC, p. 97 and below, pp. 57–8.

[60.] A type of hand-held fire arm, a precursor of the musket and rifle.

[61.] JDC, p. 263 and below, pp. 90–1; also p. 233; Borschberg, "Jacques de Coutre as a Source", pp. 84–5.

With regard to the Straits of Singapore, in the middle of these straits there is an island. The New Strait is on the one side of this island and the Old Strait is on the other. The island is triangular.... Your Majesty should order that a castle or fortress be built on this island, [equipped] with good pieces of artillery. One would then be able to monitor these two [Singapore] Straits, and no ship or vessel would be able to pass through the straits that could not be sunk. The [north-western] tip of this island [that is present-day Sentosa] is a natural fortification and the aforementioned its tip is made up of rock. This fortress could be built at little cost. The island has a cooling climate surrounded by leafy trees and it has excellent [fresh] water. The fortress would be very useful and could serve as a safe refuge for ships from China, both on the outward as well as on the return voyage. If our ships are under the protection of the fortress, they will be safe.

From whom or what did De Coutre want the ships to be safe? He was referring chiefly, but not exclusively, to the Dutch whom he routinely refers to as "rebels" in his memorials. He blamed them not just for harassing and plundering Portuguese shipping, but also for having disturbed regional trade and trading networks. Given the pivotal significance of the Singapore Straits in maintaining these networks of trade, it was vital to secure these shipping arteries by means of a fortification as well as by permanently deploying some oared galleys[62] to patrol the waters around the islands. Jacques explained:[63]

All these vessels and wares pass through these Straits of Singapore. All this commerce described above has been usurped by the rebels. They are the ones who today benefit from this trade. To remedy this state of affairs, and redirect trade to Melaka, Your Majesty must order that a very strong

---

[62] A type of vessel that is predominantly rowed but also aided by sail that traces its origins to ancient Greece and Rome. See also JDC, p. 323; SMS, p. 333.

[63] JDC, p. 229 and below, pp. 77, 79.

fortress or citadel be built in the Straits of Singapore, with a good garrison and good artillery, munitions and supplies as is advisable. The residents of the citadel could also acquire supplies from the vessels that pass through these straits, both from those that sail towards Melaka as well as those that are going to Aceh....

For the purpose of [maintaining] this commerce, Your Majesty must maintain in the [Singapore] Straits five or six well-armed Manila galleys, [that be] placed under [the command of] the citadel to patrol the straits.[64]

As intimated above, Jacques also advised the construction of a second fortification, this time on the main island of Singapore, which he called *Isla de la Sabandaria Vieja* and estimated to be about seven [marine] *leguas* long.[65] He describes the island as "situated in the Johor River estuary" and "bordered by the Old Strait" to the south and the Teberau Strait in the north.[66] The exact location for this second fortification is not as clear as the first. He described the location as a "promontory" located near the Johor River estuary, which is located about three [marine] *leguas* from the proposed first fortification on Sentosa.[67] The only possible promontory would be the area around present-day Changi Point, then known from the maps penned by Manuel Godinho de Erédia as *Tanjung Ruça* [or *Rusa*].[68]

---

64. JDC, p. 232.
65. Depending on the *legua* De Coutre had in mind, between about 38 and 43 kilometres.
66. Similar to De Coutre's contemporaries, Jan Huyghen van Linschoten and Manuel Godinho de Erédia, Singapore Island was seen to be situated between two arms or branches of the great Johor River. SMS, pp. 264–5n56; J.H. van Linschoten, *Itinerario. Voyage ofte Schipvaert van Jan Huygen van Linschoten naer Oost ofte Portugaels Indien, 1579–1592*, and *Reys-geschrift vande navigatiën der Portugaloysers*, ed. H. Kern and J.C.M. Warnsinck, 2nd ed. (The Hague: Martinus Nijhoff, 1939), IV, p. 95.
67. JDC, p. 234.
68. JDC, p. 234 and below, p. 82.

> It is necessary to build a second fortress or citadel in the Johor River estuary at the promontory of the *Isla de la Sabandaría Vieja*. This island is situated in the Johor River estuary and is bordered by the Old Strait and Teberau Strait.[69] This [second] fortress should be located about 3 [marine] leguas from the first fortress at the Singapore Straits.[70] …The [second] citadel situated at the Johor River and the [first one] at the Singapore Straits can lend each other assistance either by sea or by land.… At this [second] location Your Majesty must order a citadel to be built like to the first one that has been mentioned above.

A third, smaller fortification was proposed for a location off present-day Pulau Tekong Besar. Jacques does not go into any further commentary on this third fortification. Its function was surely to monitor traffic on the Johor River. And traffic the river certainly had: "The [Johor] River is very wide and beautiful. Ships laden with wares can enter and exit without any danger up to ten or even 12 [marine] *leguas* upstream."[71]

In setting out to construct the proposed forts, however, De Coutre advised caution. He foresaw trouble, notably from the Dutch, who, on learning of the plans to construct fortifications in the Singapore Straits region, would immediately recognise the dangers to their interest and undertake everything in their power to scupper the project. It was therefore imperative to move swiftly, entrench oneself quickly at the desired locations, and deploy a fleet that would guard and protect the building site[72] until the fortifications were complete.[73]

[69.] The Teberau or Johor Strait separates the main island of Singapore from the present-day State of Johor in Malaysia.

[70.] De Coutre appears to have had marine *leguas* in mind here; between about 17 and 19 kilometres.

[71.] Depending on the *legua* De Coutre had in mind, between 66 and 74 kilometres. See also Borschberg, "Jacques de Coutre as a Source", p. 87.

[72.] JDC, p. 238.

[73.] JDC, pp. 232–3 and below, p. 80; Borschberg, "Jacques de Coutre as a Source", p. 83.

Contemporary photograph of the north-western tip of Sentosa, named *Surgidera* point by De Coutre. (Private collection, Peter Borschberg)

When our armada[74] arrives at this place to build this citadel, it will then be necessary to entrench oneself at the aforementioned [Surgídera] point with sacks of earth, and place the artillery in the middle according to the manner and design of the citadel to be built. There is no lack of wood there to entrench oneself while one prepares materials to build the fortification. There is no lack of stone there either and [there are] lots of white stones from the sea called [*batu*] *karang*,[75] which are like limestone or gypsum. There is also a lot of firewood to burn after having made provisions for materials. [The men of the armada] will then be able to begin constructing the walls and the bulwarks and whatever else is advisable. When they finish a bulwark, they can begin to build another, so that they are always entrenched [and prepared] for anything unforeseen. For this and other purposes Your Majesty must dispatch engineers who are well versed in [building] fortifications.

As fate and history would have it, none of the fortifications proposed by Jacques de Coutre were ever built, nor did the king of Spain and Portugal acquire sovereignty over the island or found a colony on Singapore. As Zakir Hussain so aptly surmised in his review of 18 January 2014, the absence of any follow-through of these plans on part of the Iberian crowns might have been the result of neglect or more pressing problems. One is indeed left wondering: "What if those forts *had* been built?"[76]

Batu Sawar

Let us now move our attention north-eastwards from Singapore Island to the Johor River region. We know from Jacques's *Vida* that he did business in Batu Sawar on several occasions. At the time Batu Sawar served as the Johorese royal capital and was located in the upper reaches of the Johor River not far from present-day Kota

---

74. Portuguese and Spanish term for navy or fleet.
75. This is the Malay term for coral. See JDC, p. 326.
76. Zakir Hussain, "Rare Look", *The Straits Times*, 18 January 2014, D17.

Tinggi. His last (admittedly unscheduled) visit must have taken place during the final weeks of 1602 or in the first weeks of 1603.[77] As exciting and nail-biting his story of hostage-taking, cold-blooded murder and political intrigue may sound to us today, let us focus on what Jacques had to say about Batu Sawar as a key regional trading centre. He seemed to be well aware of the complete destruction of the capital Johor Lama in a military campaign led by Dom Paulo de Lima Pereira in 1587.[78] The details of the Portuguese campaign can be found in a letter written by Dom Paulo to King Philip II/I of Spain and Portugal in November 1587 and is featured as one of the appendices in my earlier book *The Singapore and Melaka Straits*.[79] Though Johor Lama is reported to have been quickly reconstructed by the Johorese,[80] the royal administrative centre was subsequently moved further upstream as a way of protecting the court from future attacks by the Portuguese and Johor's other enemies. Of this

---

[77.] This would have been just before the Dutch Admiral Jacob van Heemskerck had left Patani and headed for the Johor River region where he co-operated with the Johorese in capturing the Portuguese carrack *Santa Catarina* in the area of the Singapore Straits and the Johor River estuary. See especially Borschberg, "The Seizure of the *Santa Catarina* off Singapore: Dutch Freebooting, the Portuguese Empire and Intra-Asian Trade at the Dawn of the Seventeenth Century", *Revista de Cultura*, International Edition 11 (2004): 11–25. See also Borschberg, "The Seizure of the *Santa Catarina* Revisited: The Portuguese Empire in Asia, VOC Politics and the Origins of the Dutch-Johor Alliance (c. 1602-1616)", *JSEAS* 33, 1 (2002): 31–62.

[78.] See also the account of this incident in Ian A. MacGregor, "Johore Lama in the Sixteenth Century", *JMBRAS* 28, 2 (1955): 48–125; also MacGregor, "Notes on the Portuguese in Malaya", *JMBRAS* 28, 2 (1955): 5–47; and Manuel Lobato, *Política e Comércio dos Portugueses na Insulíndia: Malaca e as Molucas de 1575 a 1605* (Macau: Instituto Português do Oriente, 1999), pp. 198–9.

[79.] SMS, appendix II, pp. 209–28.

[80.] Pinto, *Portugueses e Malaios: Malaca e os Sultanatos de Johor e Achém, 1575–1619* (Lisbon: Sociedade Histórica da Independência de Portugal, 1997), appendix V, pp. 271–2 and its English translation as PSM, document V, pp. 287–9. See the letter of the viceroy to the king of Portugal concerning Johor's resurgence after the destruction of Johor Lama by Paulo de Lima Pereira, dated 23 November 1587; see also the letter from the *bendahara* of Melaka, Dom Henrique, to Philip I of Portugal concerning the plans by the efforts of the Johor Sultan to construct a new (or reconstruct a) fortress dated 6 February 1589; in Pinto, *Portugueses e Malaios*, appendix V, pp. 271–2 and in PSM, pp. 287–8.

move as well as on the founding of the new capital Batu Sawar, Jacques recorded:[81]

> The king of the city of Johor Lama fled and went to live on the island of Bintan, and later returned and built another city, [located] 14 [marine] *leguas* upstream,[82] which is called Batu Sawar, [but which] the Portuguese call "New Johor".…
>
> One can note that the city they call Johor Lama was destroyed by Dom Paulo de Lima [Pereira], as I have stated before, and this success will undoubtedly have been recorded in the chronicles pertaining to India. The king [of Johor] used to have his court in this city. [The settlement] that was built after the city of Johor Lama was ruined is called Batu Sawar. Today we call this other city New Johor. It is a port frequented by many carracks from diverse nations.… It has a beautiful river and a port with many large and small ships, and it is a land where merchants do vast volumes of trade and there are abundant provisions.[83]

The most important testimony about Batu Sawar, however, is a short statement that attests to its role as a key commercial centre at the turn of the 16th and 17th centuries. Singapore's own port at the time would have been interlinked with this lively riverine traffic that was invariably connected with the sea and seaborne trade:[84]

> In the aforementioned city of [Batu Sawar], there are *many* people who make a living *only* from merchandise and [from] sailing from one land to another.

[81.] JDC, p. 235 and below, pp. 84, 53–4; Borschberg, "Jacques de Coutre as a Source", pp. 90–1.
[82.] Depending on the *legua* De Coutre had in mind, between about 77 and 87 kilometres.
[83.] JDC, pp. 92–4; Borschberg, "Jacques de Coutre as a Source", p. 86.
[84.] JDC, p. 241 and below, p. 88. Emphases are mine.

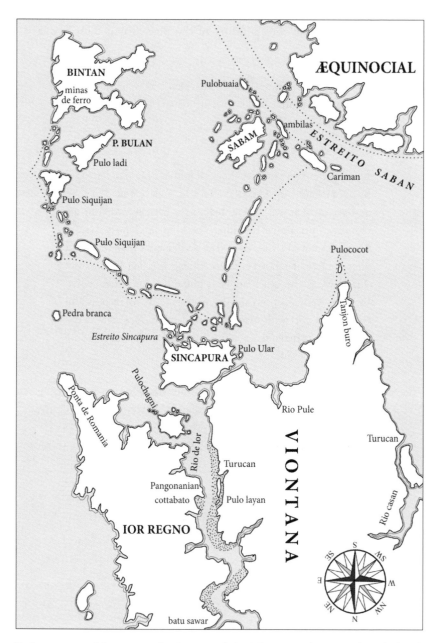

Redrawn map of Singapore, the Straits and the Johor River by Manoel Godinho de Erédia, c. 1613. This map corresponds to fol. 45 of his *Description of Melaka*.

Evidently, apart from being a base and meeting place for merchants from across the region, Batu Sawar generated enough wealth by trade that this was reflected in the way the local inhabitants carried themselves and dressed. De Coutre, who was always a keen observer of people and places, had this to say about the Johor locals:[85]

> The native people dress in the same manner as the inhabitants of the kingdom of Pahang. They are Malays by blood and very smartly dressed.

Just how well the Malays—both men and women—habitually dressed features in book I, chapter IV of the *Vida*. Recounting his visit to Pahang by sea in 1594, De Coutre was evidently impressed by the smart and tasteful dressing sense of the locals there as well, and with reference to the Malays of Batu Sawar, noted that they dressed in about the same manner. His description of the men and women of Pahang reads thus:[86]

> The natives are Muslims, however they are very tactful in their dealings and in their manner of dress. [The men] wear shirts made of *cassa* or *beatilha*[87] dyed in various colours—they call them *bajus*[88]—and as shorts they were dyed half-*beatilha*, which are made for this purpose along the Coromandel Coast, and they wrap it around between their legs in such a way that they look like shorts. They wear another white or coloured scarf as a turban, twisted like a shawl, and they carry a keris in their belt as a dagger. Some of them have a keris with a golden

---

85. JDC, pp. 93–4 and below, p. 54.
86. JDC, pp. 81–2; Borschberg, "Jacques de Coutre as a Source", p. 92.
87. A lightly woven, semi-transparent cotton textile (muslin). This was commonly used by women as veils and also by men as turbans. See JDC, pp. 305, 314.
88. This is the Malay word for shirt; sometimes also jacket. See also JDC, p. 303.

hilt, and others have a wooden hilt, according to what each individual can afford.

The women also wear a long and narrow blouse which allows a glimpse of their flesh. Some textiles are coloured, others are blue, and you find them in all colours. [They wear] a short tight jacket, which is tailored from very thin material often with elaborate designs and colours. They also tie back their hair in a very curious fashion with multi-coloured ribbons. As they walk barefoot they wear rings on both their fingers and their toes and are very beautiful in their overall appearance.

Now Jacques was most certainly not the only European author at the time to underscore the significance of Batu Sawar as a commercial emporium. Presented here are three relevant but little-known sources that have never before been translated into English. The first is a commercial report written by the Dutchman Stalpaert van der Wiele around 1600 and is thus contemporaneous with Jacques's time in Southeast Asia. His testimony translated from the original Dutch reads:[89]

> [Batu Sawar] is a *famous trading city* and is situated on the southernmost tip of the mainland of Melaka at 2 degrees north of the equator where there is also a *lot* of pepper.... This is the land where the proper Malay language has its origin. Melaka rightly belongs to [this] king. He is a very magnanimous king and is greatly respected by the foreigners. (The reference to the "king" is to Ali Jalla bin Abdul Jalil Shah of Johor who died in or around 1597. Emphases in italics are mine.)

[89.] JO, III, pp. 149–63, esp. p. 153. Translated from the original Dutch. Emphases in the text are mine.

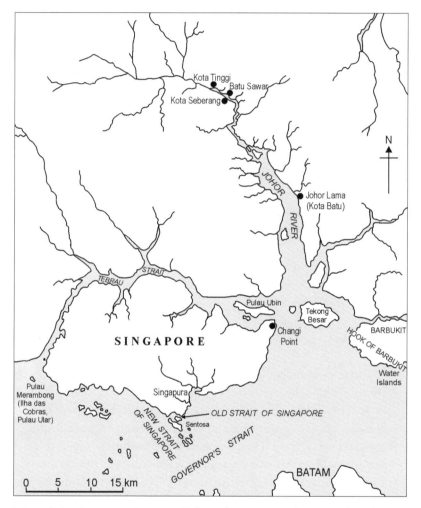

Map of the Singapore Straits and the Johor River with some of its historic upstream towns.

The second source is the "Description of the Forts and Ports of the Estado da Índia Oriental" mentioned earlier. Toward the end of its description of Melaka, the text reads in English translated from the original Portuguese:[90]

> The port of Johor is located inside Romania Point,[91] where *many* vessels are built; it has *many* provisions, eaglewood[92] and pitch; the city of Bintan is [located] on the opposite shore of that coast, well-fortified as compared to Aceh … [Batu Sawar] does a *great deal of trade*. (Emphases in italics are mine.)

Writing at the end of the 17th century, the VOC historian Pieter van Dam highlighted the significance of Batu Sawar as a port and centre of trade, though he admitted that the lands of Johor in themselves yielded very little in terms of food or produce. His observation translates from the original Dutch as follows:[93]

> From the beginning the [Dutch] Company maintained a factory in Johor, [a kingdom] which borders the land of Melaka; not that [Johor] is a land that has, or can deliver, much of itself, but in that it is *well-situated for trade*, and it *always had a lot of maritime traffic*. (Emphases in italics are mine.)

These testimonies dating from the late 16th and early 17th centuries highlight the same or very similar observations: Batu Sawar "always had a *lot* of maritime traffic" and did "a *great* deal of trade" because it was home to *many merchants* engaged in the long-distance carrying trade. But there was certainly more to it than that. It would appear that changes in trade policy, or the attitudes of individual governors in Portuguese Melaka, had the propensity to exert a serious knock-on effect for Batu Sawar's trade.

---

90. *Relação das Plantas*, p. 45.
91. The south-eastern tip of the Malay Peninsula.
92. A type of odoriferous wood drenched in its own resin that, when burned, releases a sweet, pleasant odour. See JDC, p. 318; SMS, p. 337.
93. BOC, II.1, p. 328.

Moreover, the Portuguese are reported to have done brisk business at Batu Sawar. Jacques explained the situation in the following passage:[94]

> When the Javanese come to know that in Melaka there is some captain who mistreats them—as sometimes has been the case—though their course is through the Strait of Kundur[95] to Melaka, they go from inside and around the islands in search of the island of Bintan, and then they go to Johor.[96] These vessels come laden with nutmeg, mace,[97] cloves and other merchandise. The Portuguese then go from Melaka to Johor, with cloth to sell, and buy spices and other commodities and [then] return to Melaka.

The Portuguese helped Batu Sawar flourish, a point also advanced by Paulo J. de Sousa Pinto in his study of late 16th and early 17th century Johor and its relations with Melaka.[98] Johor was well situated for trade and very competitive. Perhaps this is one of the reasons why the Portuguese launched raids on Johor's maritime and riverine settlements: to destroy Johor's rivalling ports and trading infrastructure.

As said, De Coutre's last visit to Batu Sawar in late 1602 or early 1603 coincided with a series of Portuguese coastal raids on Johor as well as a hostage crisis connected to this raiding campaign. On the return voyage from Patani, during which Jacques lost all his belongings—indeed his entire fortune at the time—to Dutch saboteurs, there was arguably also an unscheduled diplomatic

---

94. JDC, pp. 227–8 and below, p. 77.
95. See the list of place names (*Strait of Kundur*).
96. This is to say that the ships come from the Strait of Kundur or Melaka from the west and look for Bintan's double-peaked mountain, which served as a key navigational landmark in the early modern period. Once the ships reach the coast of Bintan they can then also turn north and enter into the Johor River.
97. A layer of skin separating the fruit of the nutmeg from the kernel. Mace has a slightly different flavor from nutmeg and for this reason was historically marketed as a separate spice.
98. Pinto, *Portugueses e Malaios*; also its revised translation as PSM.

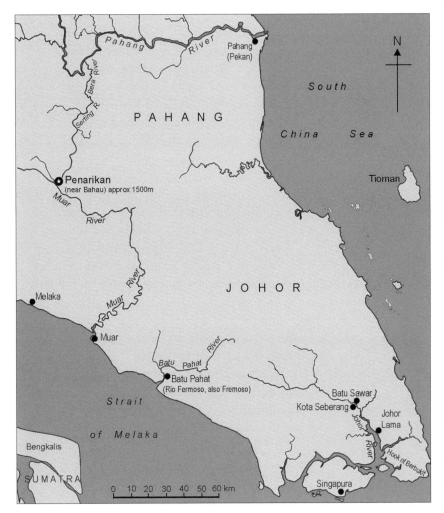

Map of the southern portion of the Malay Peninsula between Singapore and Melaka (west) and Pahang (east).

venture at the Batu Sawar court that is recounted in chapter XIX of the *Vida*.[99] This was an impromptu affair, and Jacques clearly stumbled into a crisis situation during which he offered to make himself useful in the role as messenger and mediator. One of the key persons in this event is Khoja Ibrahim, who is described as something of a resident ambassador of Portuguese Melaka in Batu Sawar.[100] Most unfortunately we do not seem to know very much about him, other than that he was a merchant with business interests in Johor and maintained a residence about a half a [land] *legua*[101]—or about a kilometre—from the palace at Batu Sawar. Jacques explained:[102]

> I arrived at the house of Ambassador [Khoja Ibrahim], who lived half a legua away from the city; he was extremely happy to see me. At that time he was conversing with two heathen merchants from Melaka, one of whom was called Nina Gadin and the other was called Nina Aure,[103] about dispatching them to Melaka with a letter for the captain [of Melaka, Fernão de Albuquerque], lodging complaints about the captain-major of the armada [Da Silva de Meneses]. I told him to send me with the letters instead because in Melaka they would give me more credence than the heathens.[104] He agreed with what I said [and] he wrote the letter immediately. Once the letter had been written, we all went to speak to the king's brother, who was called Raja Bongsu.[105] The ambassador told him how he wished to send me to Melaka. I gifted [the raja] some boxes

---

99. JDC, pp. 180–5.
100. JDC, p. 181.
101. About one kilometre.
102. JDC, p. 182 and below, pp. 61–2.
103. Nina is an honorific title in the Tamil language.
104. A reference to Nina Aure and Nina Gadin who would have been Hindus.
105. The Malay term *bongsu* means the youngest; this refers to the youngest of four brothers at the Johor court. Raja Bongsu acted and had signed himself as co-ruler. On the identity of these four princes, see CMJ, p. 160; Borschberg, *Hugo Grotius, the Portuguese and Free Trade in the East Indies* (Singapore: NUS Press, 2011), appendix 13, pp. 211–5. See also the glossary (*Raja Bongsu*).

and some glass items imploring him to ask his brother, the king [Ala'uddin Ri'ayat Shah, III], to give me permission to leave. He promised to do so and was very happy to have received the glass items. He bid me farewell, saying that we should wait for him at the king's residence.

Jacques was eventually released on the grounds that he had no significant goods or property to his name. Somewhat belated he then headed in the company of the two aforementioned merchants Nina Aure and Nina Gadin for Melaka. As he was proceeding downstream toward the Singapore Strait he crossed paths with Júlio de Barros around Johor Lama, the old Johor capital located in the lower reaches of the Johor River not far from Singapore. Júlio was just returning from Melaka with a note for the king of Johor from the captain-major of the armada, Da Silva de Meneses. He implored Jacques to wait for him there at Johor Lama and insisted that he would be arriving with his fully-laden junk shortly. But sensing that the situation was deteriorating very rapidly, and after witnessing how a group of merchants from Melaka were mobbed and killed by the local population at Johor Lama, Jacques and his fellow travellers decided it was best to move on immediately. That, on hindsight, proved to be a life-saving decision. For when Júlio handed the reply of the captain-major of the armada to the Batu Sawar court (the exact content of which remains unknown), the Johorese officials decided to kill all the Portuguese and Melakan prisoners who were being held captive by the *shahbandar*.[106] Jacques reminisced in his *Vida* years later with evident anguish: "If I had been there I would undoubtedly have perished with all the others."[107] With the slaughtering of these estimated 150 Portuguese and Christian captives at Batu Sawar, Jacques's urgent mission to act as a go-between of the Melaka captain, ambassador Khoja Ibrahim and the Batu Sawar court had lapsed.

[106.] The Malay port master who also held jurisdiction over foreign merchants. See also the glossary (*shahbandar*).

[107.] JDC, p. 184.

Conclusions

What does De Coutre yield to the contemporary reader of Singapore and Johor history? The texts give further endorsement to the view that Singapore has always been at the crossroads of major trading routes. It was not a place long-forgotten by time—at least not in the late 1500s and early 1600s—but a place very much at the forefront of attention of the early European colonial powers. In the period of De Coutre, Singapore was seen as an island in the estuary of the Johor River, and in the upper reaches of this great river there were a series of settlements that included the former royal residence and fortification at Johor Lama (destroyed in 1587 by the Portuguese) as well as a new capital and administrative centre at Batu Sawar, located not far from present-day Kota Tinggi. The islands are said to have been inhabited by *saletes* (*orang laut*) and Malays who were loyal to the king of Johor. Singapore also had a settlement, named by Jacques *Sabandaría*—after the presence of a *shahbandar* or port master, just as on the maps drawn during De Coutre's lifetime by Manuel Godinho de Erédia. And Singapore was reportedly home to one of the best ports in the East Indies. De Coutre provides a unique and historically valuable account of the maritime traffic using the New and the Old Straits of Singapore. The island was clearly located along a busy and strategically important maritime artery. But the waters around Singapore and especially in the straits were treacherous and challenging even to the most experienced mariners. Passing ships arriving from the west used to wait off the north-western tip of Sentosa for the winds and the currents to change. The *orang laut* who were active in the waters around Singapore, moreover, pulled up to the side of these waiting ships to sell fish, fruit, fresh water and handicraft such as parasols made from palm leaves. Jacques explained that crews were careful and wary when dealing with the *orang laut*, and that these people of the sea lived with animals and family on their small boats. They bartered their produce and goods for rice, metal pieces and fabrics, including old blankets. Because ships often had to wait for days for the right sailing conditions to prevail, present-day Sentosa was almost certainly better known than Singapore Island as it served these waiting crews and passing ships as a place to fetch fresh water.

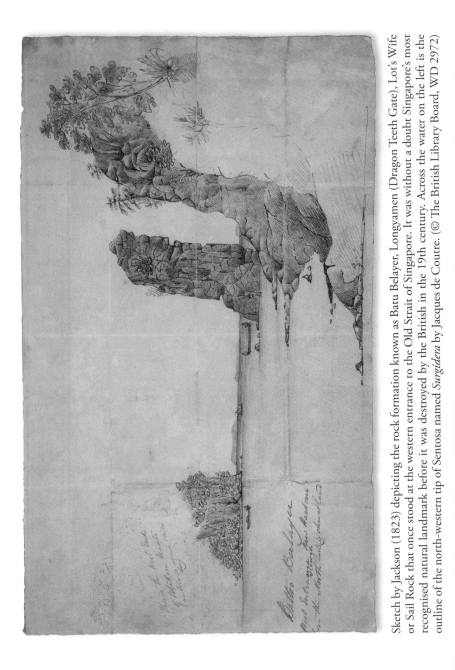

Sketch by Jackson (1823) depicting the rock formation known as Batu Belayer, Longyamen (Dragon Teeth Gate), Lot's Wife or Sail Rock that once stood at the western entrance to the Old Strait of Singapore. It was without a doubt Singapore's most recognised natural landmark before it was destroyed by the British in the 19th century. Across the water on the left is the outline of the north-western tip of Sentosa named *Surgidera* by Jacques de Coutre. (© The British Library Board, WD 2972)

Most important of all, De Coutre had recognised the strategic significance of the Singapore Straits. The island we now know as Sentosa played an important part in his calculation. He singled out a location on the north-western tip of the island at the site of present-day Fort Siloso, built by the British, as a first recommended location for a citadel or fortification with which the Iberian powers could control the flow of maritime traffic through the Straits. Another location was singled out along the east coast, probably near Changi, as well as a third location on an islet or shoal just located off Pulau Tekong Besar. These two latter fortifications were meant to monitor shipping through the Teberau Straits and also up and down the Johor River. From the eastern coast of Singapore it would have also been possible to see ships entering or leaving the Riau Strait between the present-day Indonesian islands of Batam and Bintan.

It was De Coutre's vision and recommendation that the king of Spain and Portugal acquire Singapore Island and found a European colony to leverage on its excellent port and boost trade. The proposed forts, however, were never built and the Iberian colony on Singapore was never founded. We do not know for sure why De Coutre's plans did not come to fruition in the intended manner. But he had formulated and expounded clear plans with a clear vision that today can crucially serve to debunk a stubbornly entrenched myth: that from the latter middle ages and across the whole of the early modern era, Singapore had remained an essentially forgotten and neglected place, unseen and unrecognised until the arrival of the British about 1800. There can be no doubt that Jacques de Coutre's writings evidence as well as underscore Singapore's long-acknowledged strategic location as well as its immensely promising potential as a port and colonial settlement situated at a critical nodal point of busy international shipping routes.

The Life of
Jacques de Coutre

The journey I made to the kingdom of Pahang in the year 1594 and the events that I experienced

In the first two chapters of his autobiography or *Vida*, Jacques de Coutre explains how after a brief stint fishing for cod in the North Sea, he and his brother Joseph decided to enlist as soldiers and head to the East Indies. Both young men arrived in Goa, but Joseph fell ill from the long voyage to India and needed to convalesce. Jacques then headed for Melaka alone, arriving in September 1593. Immediately upon his arrival, he was taken under the wing of an ageing gem dealer who was originally from Venice but was already living for some time in Melaka. This man became his patron and introduced him to key persons in Melaka. The story picks up with the statement that, six months after his arrival, he made his first trip to Pahang via Singapore.

Six months later I went to the kingdom of Pahang on the orders of Captain[1] Francisco da Silva de Meneses, not just to accompany an embassy that he was sending in the name of Your Majesty to that kingdom but also to buy diamonds and bezoars,[2] because I had some knowledge of such wares. From that point onwards I began

---

[1.] The captain (governor) of Portuguese Melaka. See also the glossary (*captain*).
[2.] See the glossary (*bezoar*).

to make my fortune, being a soldier and merchant whenever an occasion presented itself. I set sail aboard his own ship accompanied by Martim Teixeira, which was the ambassador's name, who served as the captain of the ship. As the Southern Sea[3] is never free from storms, as soon as we left the port we ran into a tempest that obliged us to enter into the Batu Pahat River,[4] which is nearby, [and] where we rode out the storm. The following day we unfurled our sails and we passed the islands Pulau Pisang[5] [and] Pulau Karimun,[6] [located] near the Strait[s] of Singapore. [The area around Singapore] is completely covered with large and leafy trees, so much so that when ships pass by the tips of their yards inevitably brush along the branches, especially in the Old Strait [of Singapore].[7] The passage is very narrow, and there is a great deal of [maritime] traffic with many ships from different kingdoms.

Many fishermen live along these straits, who are called *saletes*.[8] While pointing out the strait to us they came aboard our ship with fresh fish and a lot of local fruits, which are very different from the fruits in Europe and which they pick in the hills. Some are called durians, and others are called mangosteens, and others are called *rambai* and *buah duku*;[9] they are very healthy and tasty. They brought us many parasols made from palm leafs—they call them *payones*[10]—and fresh water. They gave us everything in exchange for rice and old fabrics. They are extremely poor people. They live in some sloops that are at most five or six *varas*[11] long, and they are very narrow, made of thin, light planks, and on them they have their homes with wives and children, dogs, cats, [and] even hens

---

[3.] Broadly the seas of the East Indies; present-day Southeast Asia. See also the list of place names (*South*).
[4.] The (old) Portuguese name for the Batu Pahat River, which spills into the sea at the south-western coast of the Malay Peninsula. See JDC, p. 378.
[5.] See the list of place names (*Pulau Pisang*).
[6.] See the list of place names (*Karimun*).
[7.] See the list of place names (*Old Strait of Singapore*).
[8.] That is *orang laut* or sea-gypsies. See also the glossary (*orang laut, saletes*).
[9.] A fruit known as *langsat*.
[10.] The term *payung* is Malay for parasol.
[11.] About five to six metres.

with their chicks. They raise everything there inside the little sloop, which I was amazed to see because the boats are so narrow. When they go fishing the man sits on the *perahu* with a harpoon and the wife and children paddle very fast and very skilfully. Very old men can be found among them; I met some who said that all of them were a hundred years old. They are treacherous people by nature. For this reason we deal with them very carefully and with weapons in our hands, because it has happened that they were allowed to come aboard our ships in such numbers, ostensibly to sell fresh fish, and in the blink of an eye they rose and killed everyone aboard the ship. As arms they carry some poisoned daggers, which they call *kerisses*, and spears made of wild palm, without any iron. They are called *seligis*[12] and they throw them so hard that they can even penetrate an iron breastplate and any shield no matter how sturdy they are. Finally we passed through the Old Strait, which the king of Johor had ordered be obstructed when Dom Paulo de Lima Pereira, captain of Melaka, captured the city of Johor from him;[13] however, with the passage of time and the force of the currents it is now no longer blocked. We anchored in front of a place called *Sabandaría*[14] which is inhabited by Malays, subjects of the said king of Johor, to whom the *saletes*, who sail in the straits, [also] pay tribute.

We once again set sail and after passing by the island of Tioman[15] and that of Tinggi[16] and other islands, we arrived at the kingdom of Pahang.[17] One can note that the main city, in which the court is located, is also called Pahang, just like the kingdom. We entered by going upriver until we arrived at a small place that is called Beruas[18] [and] we anchored there. In this place they make a lot

---

12.　See the glossary (*seligi*).
13.　This refers to the events of 1587. See SMS, appendix 2, pp. 209–28.
14.　Settlement around the house or compound of the *shahbandar* of Singapura. See also the list of place names (*Sabandaria*).
15.　See the list of place names (*Tioman*).
16.　One of the islands located off the eastern coast of Johor State in Malaysia, located to the south of Tioman. See JDC, p. 377.
17.　See the list of place names (*Pahang*).
18.　See the list of place names (*Beruas*).

of wine from *nipa* [*palm*][19]—which are certain trees in those lands that grow along the water [and] which appear quite similar to wild date palms; the wine is like *aguardente*.[20] They told me later that in the woods nearby there were many wild boars. As I like to hunt, I went ashore that night out of curiosity, under the moonlight, accompanied by two soldiers, and in the woods I built a makeshift shack out of branches so as to be able to shoot from there. I killed a very large wild boar. As it was Friday, I ordered that it be salted and put into four large earthenware jars. The following day we weighed anchor and we dropped anchor again in front of the main square of the city of Pahang.

---

[19] The juice or water of the palm, when left to ferment, produces arak. Its leaves are used for roofing and is called *atap* in Malay. See JDC, pp. 303, 331.
[20] A fermented or distilled alcoholic beverage which is usually clear. See JDC, p. 300.

Chapter VI

About the voyage I made from Melaka to the kingdom of Johor in 1594 and what happened to me

Shortly after returning from his first major trip to Pahang just a few months after his arrival in Melaka in September 1593, Jacques de Coutre undertook a second voyage, this time to Batu Sawar. This was apparently his first of several trips to the Johorese royal capital located in the upper reaches of the Johor River. In the first part of the chapter he indulges in retelling the story of Luis del Castillo, a fraudster who claimed to be a relative of the king of Spain and Portugal and travelled incognito through Southeast Asia. Del Castillo managed to dupe the Johor royal court and even the captain of Melaka and the bishop before his fraud was uncovered. The second part of the chapter contains valuable information on Batu Sawar as a commercial centre at the end of the 16th century.

One month after having returned from the kingdom of Pahang I went to Johor[1] with a consignment of textiles, part of which belonged to me and the other part to the captain [of Melaka], Francisco da Silva de Meneses, to exchange them for diamonds and bezoar stones on behalf of both of us, which is what I effectively did when I arrived there.

[1.] See the list of place names (*Batu Sawar*).

It so happened that while I was there three Castilian frigates,[2] commanded by Captain Gallinato,[3] came from the kingdom of Cambodia, where they had scored a major victory. To describe the situation succinctly: since wars were raging in Cambodia as there were some uprisings, the native king [Sâtha I], taking advantage of his friendship with the Castilians, requested assistance from the governor of Manila, who sent him those frigates with very skilled people. When Captain Gallinato[4] arrived in Cambodia, believing he would find the rightful king, he found a tyrant[5] in his stead who had killed [Sâtha][6] and was obeyed by one and all as the [new] king. This tyrant wished to kill Gallinato in treachery. Having sized up the situation, the Castilians attacked. They killed a lot of people and one of the tyrant's sons.[7] After having burnt over 200 baxels[8] which he encountered in the river, [Captain Gallinato] came to the port of Johor,[9] where he remained for many days. When he decided to return to Manila, he left behind a Castilian, who had asked for permission to go to Melaka. He had a good presence, [was accompanied by] two slaves, and he was very well dressed. He disembarked with 14 chests filled with sand, which he

---

2.   The term originally refers to an open Portuguese naval craft that was often rowed and in the 16th and 17th century deployed in the East Indies. See JDC, p. 322.

3.   This is probably Juan Xuárez [Juárez] Gallinato who is mentioned by Antonio de Morga in his *Sucesos de las Islas Filipinas*, tr. and ed. J.S. Cummins (Cambridge: Cambridge University Press for the Hakluyt Society, 1971), pp. 82–5; also Subrahmanyam, "Manila, Melaka, Mylapore…: A Dominican Voyage through the Indies, ca. 1600", *Archipel* 57 (1999): 235.

4.   Concering the Gallinato expedition to Cambodia, see L.P. Briggs, "Spanish Intervention in Cambodia, 1593–1603", *T'oung Pao*, second series 39, 1/3 (1950): 132–60, esp. p. 154.

5.   Better known as the Laksamana, Oknha de Chu, a Malay and native of Johor. Briggs, "Spanish Intervention", p. 150. See also JDC, pp. 43, 125.

6.   The rightful or legitimate king.

7.   Concerning this episode, see Briggs, "Spanish Intervention", pp. 156–7.

8.   A generic Portuguese term that refers to a cargo ship or a barge. In the Malay Archipelago, the term was commonly applied as a synonym for *perahu* (see the separate entry for that vessel type), but sometimes it can also refer to a junk. See JDC, p. 305.

9.   An uncertain location, possibly Singapore or Johor Lama.

pretended were reals-of-eight[10]—he was the world's greatest liar. He immediately sent a message to the king of Johor [Raja Ali Jalla bin Abdul Jalil Shah], through one of the slaves, saying that he was Don Luis del Castillo, a relative of the King of Spain [Philip II], and that he had come to those lands incognito so as not to be recognised. He asked his permission to meet with him, since he had important matters to discuss with [the king]. Upon hearing this message, the king, believing this to be true, immediately went to look for him, accompanied by all the people in the city [of Batu Sawar] with great fanfare. When Don Luis del Castillo saw the king he presented him three emerald rings. In recognition of this gift, the king took off his sword[11] that he was wearing in his belt and gave it to him. Don Luis took it and then unfastened his [sword], which was worked in silver, and gave it to the king, who pretended that he greatly appreciated the gift. Once the greetings were over the king climbed on to a small elephant and Don Luis got on to another. He rode on the right side of the king and they were followed by four of the king's sons walking on foot,[12] with all their gentlemen, and all the city's people with their arms walked ahead of the group. In this manner they reached the king's residence with all the pomp and pageantry that one can image in that land. On this occasion they celebrated the *baxels* that were in the river with a salvo of artillery and musket-fire,[13] [everything was] festooned with flags, especially the city's[14] artillery. In the five days that Don Luis was hosted by the king he went to inspect

---

10. A silver coin minted in the Spanish Americas with a face value of eight *reals* and containing a little over 27 grams of silver. See JDC, pp. 338–9.

11. Probably a keris and not a sword.

12. Raja Ali Jalla was known to have had at least six sons, two of whom were killed after a wedding at Patani, and four who survived. The four surviving sons were 'Ala'uddin Ri'ayat Shah III, Raja Bongsu (later Abdullah Ma'ayat Shah), the Raja Siak and Raja Laut. The precise identity of the four sons mentioned by De Coutre cannot be confirmed. Concerning the sons of Raja Ali Jalla, see also GPFT, appendix 13, pp. 211–5.

13. A type of fire arm.

14. This is a reference to Batu Sawar. De Coutre explains the transfer of the royal residence from Johor Lama to Batu Sawar further below. See also the glossary (*Batu Sawar*).

the city's walls with all due ceremony, accompanied by the king [of Johor]. As the walls were made of wood, he suggested a better layout and way of placing the artillery so [that Batu Sawar could] defend [itself] against the king of Aceh,[15] who was waging a war with Johor at the time. Since the king though that the suggestion was suitable he immediately ordered that it be implemented, and after this became very friendly towards Don Luis.

After five days Don Luis asked for permission to head for Melaka, promising to return soon. He claimed to have some important issues to resolve with the captain of Melaka. Not only did the king give him permission to leave but he also provided him with a ship and 15 slaves to serve him—of which I bought two slaves. In the end he went to Melaka accompanied by many ships; I also travelled on one of them. As soon as we arrived the captain[16] and the bishop of Melaka[17] visited Don Luis, greatly honouring him. During the course of the visit Don Luis stated how he had been sent by the king of Spain and the reason why he had travelled through those lands incognito. During the four days that he was there, many festivities and processions were staged, which Don Luis attended in person, walking behind the Holy Sacrament, between the captain and the bishop, with a candle in his hand, accompanied by all of Melaka's citizens and gentlemen.

After four days he returned to Johor saying how important it was that he do so, and he took letters of recommendation from the captain and the bishop addressed to the king [of Johor],[18] declaring and attesting to the quality of Don Luis, [affirming] that he was a great nobleman, and that he was going to see His Highness. The letters requested that he be treated with all the due deference that his person merited. When he arrived in Johor, the king saw that he had returned accompanied by many Portuguese and [bearing]

---

15. Raja Buyong of Aceh.
16. Here and subsequently a reference to the captain of Melaka, Francisco da Silva de Meneses.
17. Here and subsequently a reference to Dom João Ribeiro Gaio, the Bishop of Melaka. Concerning the career of this controversial cleric, see the brief exposé in PSM, pp. 198–200.
18. Raja Ali Jalla bin Abdul Jalil.

the aforesaid letters. If the king had given him a grand reception on his first visit, this time he gave him an even more magnificent welcome and showered him with gifts. Three days later he again returned to Melaka, promising the king that he would send him a fleet of Portuguese to go with his fleet to wage war on the king of Aceh. As soon as Don Luis arrived in Melaka he secretly negotiated a light bantin[19] to go to Aceh. Meanwhile two ambassadors who had been sent by the king of Johor arrived, to enquire whether the fleet that Don Luis had promised the king of Johor was being prepared. When the captain [of Melaka] came to know of this promise he decided to apprehend Don Luis to know on what basis he had made such a promise. He must have suspected that this would happen and that [very] night he fled to the kingdom of Aceh, where he also duped the king with other tall stories. The king of Aceh[20] believed these yarns to be true and gave him a carrack laden with pepper and a crew of native sailors. He set sail with the carrack and the permission of the king of Aceh and went to the kingdom of Pegu.[21] On the way he mistreated the sailors, who conspired against him and killed him one night, along with all his slaves and those who were accompanying him, and they rebelled on the carrack. Only one of his slaves managed to escape, who brought us the news in Melaka.

This was the fate of Don Luis del Castillo, who said that he was a relative of the king of Spain, [but] who [in reality] had Muslim blood and had been flogged in New Spain[22] and banished from the Philippines.

Having become distracted with the story of this charlatan I have not yet written of the many things I could recount about the kingdom of Johor. One can note that the city they call Johor

---

[19.] A Malay craft often used in the 16th and 17th centuries in naval warfare. It was propelled by breast oars and featured two rudders and two masts. See JDC, p. 304; SMS, p. 331.

[20.] Raja Buyong of Aceh.

[21.] Home in earlier centuries to a Mon kingdom, Pegu served in the early 17th century as the capital of a kingdom ruled by the Taungoo dynasty ("Burma") until 1635.

[22.] A reference to the Spanish administrative unit in the Americas broadly corresponding with today's Mexico.

Lama[23] was destroyed by Dom Paulo de Lima [Pereira],[24] as I have stated before,[25] and this success will undoubtedly have been recorded in the chronicles pertaining to India. The king [of Johor] used to have his court in this city. [The settlement] that was built after the city of Johor Lama was ruined is called Batu Sawar. Today we call this other city New Johor. It is a port frequented by many carracks from diverse nations. The native people dress in the same manner as the inhabitants of the kingdom of Pahang.[26] They are Malays by blood and very smartly dressed. As arms they use lances, *harquebuses*,[27] spears, swords, *rodelas*,[28] *kerisses* that are typical of the Minangkabau[29] people—which is what they are called—and artillery. It has a beautiful river and a port with many large and small ships, and it is a place where merchants do vast volumes of trade and there are abundant provisions. The king is called Raja Ali [Jalla bin Abdul Jalil]. His grandfather was once the king of Melaka,[30] which was an ancient city that spanned 12 [marine] *leguas* along the coast.[31] He titled himself "Emperor of the Malays".[32] After his death the empire began to crumble and is now completely extinguished. The most important monarch in the East Indies today is [the king] of Aceh. After I returned to Melaka I went on other journeys, which I have not described since nothing noteworthy happened to me that would merit being recorded.

---

23. See the list of place names (*Johor Lama*).
24. Concerning the epistolary report of Dom Paulo de Lima Pereira's attack on, and destruction of, Johor Lama in 1587, see SMS, pp. 212–28.
25. At the end of chapter III.
26. This had been described at the beginning of chapter IV.
27. A fire arm common in the 16th and 17th centuries. *Harquebuses* were based on a German-manufactured precursor and resembled later firearms such as the musket and the rifle. See JDC, p. 324.
28. A type of shield. See JDC, p. 339.
29. Name of a polity and people in the central-western highlands of Sumatra. The Minangkabau were known for their pepper and gold dust. See JDC, p. 368.
30. In the time of the Melaka Sultanate before its fall to the Portuguese in 1511.
31. Between about 66 and 74 kilometres.
32. Concerning this title, see also SMS, pp. 226, 323n155; GPFT, pp. 365–6n83.

Chapter VII

How I went to the kingdom of Siam, accompanying an embassy that the captain of Melaka sent in the name of His Majesty. What happened to us until we reached the port of this kingdom in the year 1595

This marks the first of several chapters touching on Jacques de Coutre's eight-month trip to Ayutthaya, where he had been sent as a member of a diplomatic delegation to the court of Siam's great King Naresuan. On their way to the Siamese capital, the ships carrying Jacques and the Portuguese emissaries passed through the Singapore Strait. The short excerpt yields important information on how ships arriving at the Old Strait of Singapore had to wait for the proper weather and tidal conditions to pass through and make their onward voyage. Jacques's account also testifies to the fact that present-day Sentosa was a well-known watering hole where passing ships would fetch fresh water.

After I had returned to Melaka from Johor it so happened that King [Naresuan] of Siam captured the kingdom and the city of Cambodia,[1] where there was a Christian community, many

---

[1.] This is a reference to the Cambodian capital Lovek, which had been attacked by King Naresuan (Phra Naret) of Siam in 1593.

Portuguese, Franciscan, Augustinian and Dominican convents as well as clergymen. All of them were captured and taken to Siam along with all the finest things in that kingdom. Among the Dominican friars there was one who was called Friar Jorge da Mota, an astute but terrible man, who managed to become friends with a personal servant of the king who was called Phra Choduk.[2] By means of the gifts he gave him, [Da Mota] convinced the king to send him to Melaka with letters for the captain so as to negotiate a peace agreement with the Portuguese. Friar Jorge arrived with the letters in Melaka, he handed them over to [Captain] Francisco da Silva de Meneses and he informed him about the state of the Portuguese in Siam. Then, in order to get [the captain] to do his bidding [Da Mota] sought to tempt him by appealing to his greed. He claimed that in Siam textiles were worth a lot of money and that there were many rubies, sapphires and many other precious stones and riches that King [Naresuan] had captured in Cambodia and in the wars with Pegu. [These had been taken] in such large quantities that they were sold by the *chupo*[3]—which is a weight like half a *celamin*[4] used in Siam to measure rice, vegetables and other provisions. To corroborate his words [Da Mota] showed [the captain] some ruby rings, which, according to him, he had bought very cheaply and were worth a lot of money. I suspect all of this was a lie.

When Captain Francisco da Silva [de Meneses] heard this information he decided to send Friar [Jorge] and an ambassador, [Manuel Pereira de Abreu] to King [Naresuan] of Siam to arrive at a peace settlement and to free the Christians who were being held captive in that kingdom. [The captain] also ordered that [the ambassador] buy those precious stones that the friar had said were so cheap and to make the most of that occasion.

[2.]   Most likely a corruption of Phra Choduk, the head of the Port Department of the Left. See JDC, p. 335.

[3.]   A Spanish unit to measure the volume or mass of foodstuffs and equivalent to about 4.6 litres. See JDC, p. 316.

[4.]   A *chupo* is equivalent to a half a *celamine*, about 2.3 litres. See JDC, p. 315.

Very few people wished to go to Siam, since the king had the reputation of a tyrant, fickle and deceitful—and everyone who went there was motivated by greed. The captain chose one of his retainers to go there as an ambassador, along with a factor, [Simão Peres], and nine Portuguese to accompany the embassy. When things were at this stage [the captain] called me and asked me to accompany that embassy. He then also instructed me to buy some rubies and sapphires there on his behalf. I refused and excused myself as much as I could; [but] it proved impossible not to go. In the end the captain made an agreement with me in the presence of Friar Jorge in order to make me more comfortable with the idea. On 8 May 1595, we set sail from the port [of Melaka] in a junk that belonged to this captain—a junk is a *baxel* that are used by the natives of the South,[5] and some of them are very large, [they can even be] a thousand *toneladas*[6] or more. Their sails are made of palm leaves. Apart from the sailors and officials who were Chinese, the people who sailed aboard the junk included the ambassador, the friar, myself and ten Portuguese; and everything on board was done in accordance to how the friar wanted things done. We reached the Strait of Singapore,[7] and they threw the *batel*[8] into the water. The friar sought to coerce me to go in this *batel* with three companions to fetch fresh water on an island that was called *Isla de Arena*.[9] We approached it; I got the water. By the time we returned night had fallen. I could not see the junk, they did not light either a lamp nor did they fire any shots, even though I made many signals. [This lasted] until the current carried me out of the New Strait [of Singapore][10] and then I saw them at anchor. At the entrance to this strait I came across some *orang laut* vessels, who attacked us in order to capture us. We repelled them, however, by means of our barrel guns, and one of

---

5.   Here meaning in Southeast Asia. See also the glossary (*South*).

6.   A unit to measure the weight of a ship's cargo as well as the mass of liquids. In Spain, it is equivalent to about 920 kilograms; in Portugal, 793 kilograms.

7.   Reference is here probably to the area around the north-western tip of present-day Sentosa off Fort Siloso.

8.   A small craft propelled by breast oars. See JDC, p. 305.

9.   Present-day Sentosa.

10.   Along the south-western coast of present-day Sentosa.

my companions was injured. We rowed the entire night until we saw the junk at dawn and we managed to reach it feeling fed up and irritated.

We could not pass through the Strait [of Singapore] with the junk because the sea was rising,[11] which tends to happen with the constellation of the moon, and the currents usually last at least two or three days. At this point, that too at night, the friar insisted we pass through [the waters]. It would have been a difficult task by day and was even more so at night. He insisted persistently until we raised anchor and the junk slammed against a rock. However, the currents only damaged the rudder, which was shattered into two thousand splinters. [The rock] struck the junk right in the middle. At this point we repaired [the rudder] with some *espadelas*[12] [and] with these we managed to control the junk. Thereafter, once we had passed the island of Pulau Tioman,[13] we threw [the corpse of] a comrade of mine into the sea, who had died of diarrhoea. He was a Frenchman who had been born in Avignon and his name was Don Claudio de Godon. We passed by many other islands, which I am not naming so as not to be overly verbose. We reached some uninhabited islands, which were called Pulau *Sanquiuxu*[14] and Pulau Redang.[15] We went ashore there to take on fresh water. After having fetched some water a few people began bathing and washing clothes on the shore.

[11.] That means the tide was coming in.

[12.] An oar that can also be used as a rudder.

[13.] An island off the south-eastern coast of the Malay Peninsula. For centuries Tioman was a navigational landmark for ships sailing to or from the Vietnam Coast, China and Japan.

[14.] This appears to be a corruption of the Chinese toponym *San chio hsü*, the Chinese name for Perhentian Island West. See JDC, p. 376.

[15.] A group of islands consisting of the main island Redang (sometimes also Great Redang) together with nine other islets nearby. See JDC, p. 376.

Chapter XIX

The reason why the king of Johor gave orders to kill some 50 Portuguese and many other local Christians from Melaka, from among whom two of my slaves and I escaped. A description of the same journey until I reached Melaka

Although Jacques de Coutre had already resolved by 1602 to return to Goa to wed Doña Catarina do Couto, circumstances and the lack of ships travelling to India that season did not enable him to undertake this trip immediately. On his return to Melaka from Manila, he decided to sell his cargo of spices and use the proceeds to buy cloth. The idea was to turn a quick profit on these at Patani, and so Jacques undertook his voyage in the company of one Júlio de Barros, who is described as a nephew of the bishop of Melaka. On his arrival however, he found not only that Dutch ships were waiting at anchor for cargo, but also that the situation in Patani was quickly turning against the Portuguese. Evidently at the instigation of the Dutch, the merchant António Saldanha was murdered in his home. The Dutch then drilled holes into the hull of Jacques's junk, which was waiting at anchor to set sail for Melaka. The ship sank and his cargo of rice was completely destroyed by the salt water. When it became clear that the Dutch were also out to kill him, Jacques was given refuge and help to flee by someone he calls Cik Tangan, a powerful woman in Patani who apparently had extensive business interests in commerce and shipping. After a harrowing trip aboard one of the Patani ships that was heading for Melaka, Portuguese naval patrols in and around the Singapore Straits forced the Patani vessel to call at Batu Sawar instead. This unscheduled stop brought Jacques into the centre of an unfolding crisis in Johor that ended in the slaughter of many Melaka Christians as well as his friend and companion Júlio de Barros.

When I disembarked I came across my companion Júlio de Barros and in the city [of Batu Sawar] there were some 50 or more Portuguese and many local Christians from Melaka, who told me that the monarch of that kingdom of Johor was very angry ever since the captain-major, Francisco da Silva de Meneses, had seized a junk belonging to the king and had killed an ambassador that he had sent to his brother-in-law, the king of Perak, together with everyone who was accompanying the said ambassador. The king had ordered that the captain-[major] be asked why he had committed that aggression. The answer was sent two days later. [Da Silva de Meneses][1] replied that His Highness had been misinformed and that he had not done any such thing. With this answer the king and the people calmed down, and the following day the captain-major sent seven or eight women and some barrel guns and *kerisses* with another message, saying that he had inspected his armada and had found those women and the weapons that he was sending therewith to him. They had been brought by a captain named Pantaleão Carneiro.[2] The [women and the weapons] must have been from the missing junk and, he would severely punish

---

[1.] Da Silva's name is revealed in later sections of this chapter.

[2.] This is possibly the same Portuguese named Pantaleão Carneiro, a resident of Manila, who had been a subordinate of Diogo Veloso (sometimes Beloso) and who was involved in the hearings against the king of Champa in 1593 and accompanied the embassy of King Sâtha of Cambodia to Manila. See Briggs, "Spanish Intervention", pp. 137, 148; also S. Subrahmanyam, "Manila, Melaka, Mylapore…: A Dominican Voyage through the Indies, ca. 1600", *Archipel* 57 (1999): 234, who claims that Pantaleão Carneiro was a native Portuguese from Lisbon.

the captains who had been accomplices. With the arrival of the women the people and the king[3] once again became agitated, so much so that they wanted to kill all the Christians who were [at Batu Sawar], saying that the armada had seized all the *baxels* that had set sail from that port;[4] and that was why they had not received any news from these [vessels]. Hearing this noise and commotion the king's mother came out and she managed to calm down the king's and the people's wrath, because the captain-major [Da Silva de Meneses] had sent a message saying that he guaranteed that there would be no more disturbances.

A few days later two Johorese vessels arrived from the kingdom of Pahang. The captain-major issued instructions that they were to be seized and that all the people who were sailing aboard them were to be kept in the holds of his ships. The king and the people got so upset that they apprehended all the Portuguese and the Christians from Melaka who were present in the city and took them to the house of the *shahbandar*[5]—that was what the highest official of justice was called. As soon as I saw this turmoil I went to the house of a Muslim who was a native of Melaka and was the [official] state interpreter for the captain of Melaka, [Fernão de Albuquerque]. [He had been] entrusted with negotiations to unite the armadas of the king of Johor and the Portuguese so as to capture the kingdom of Aceh, since this was something that the king of Johor ardently desired. [The king of Johor's fleet] was making the necessary preparations while the armada commanded by Francisco da Silva [de Meneses] was sailing along the coast and creating the aforementioned disturbances. I arrived at the house of Ambassador [Khoja Ibrahim],[6] who lived half a *legua* away[7] from the city; he was extremely happy to see me. At that time he was conversing with two heathen merchants from Melaka,

---

3.   Ala'uddin Ri'ayat Shah III.

4.   Batu Sawar.

5.   See the glossary (*shahbandar*).

6.   Khoja Ibrahim. *Khoja* or *Khwaja* derives from the Persian language, and in the 17th century the term was sometimes used as an equivalent or counterpart to the Portuguese *Senhor* or Dutch *Heer*; "Mister", "Sir". JDC, pp. 326–7.

7.   About one kilometre.

one of whom was called Nina Gadin and the other was called Nina Aure, about dispatching them to Melaka with [a] letter for the captain, [De Albuquerque], lodging complaints about the captain-major of the armada, [Da Silva de Meneses]. I told him to send me with the letters instead because in Melaka they would give me more credence than the heathens. He agreed with what I said [and] he wrote the letter immediately. Once the letter had been written, we all went to speak to the king's brother, who was called Raja Bongsu.[8] The ambassador told him how he wished to send me to Melaka. I gifted [the *raja*] some boxes and some glass items imploring him to ask his brother, King ['Ala'uddin], to give me permission to leave. He promised to do so and was very happy to have received the glass items. He bid me farewell, saying that we should wait for him at the king's residence. When I had made it half way there I was surrounded by many men and they apprehended me and took me to where the other Portuguese and the native, Melaka-born Christians were being held [by the *shahbandar*]. I was very annoyed because I was well aware of the fury of those people. I entrusted my soul to God, preparing myself to die along with the others.

It is important to note that six or seven days before I was imprisoned I had adopted the habit of taking a walk along the bank of the [Johor] River every night from eight o'clock to nine o'clock. Every night I used to hear a voice as though it was emanating from one of the many ships belonging to the native people of that land, which were moored along the river [bank]. The voice used to call out to me loudly in the Flemish language: "Compatriot, go on, go with God [away] from here"; this was something that left me astounded because I did not know of any Fleming or Dutchman in that place. Nor could I believe that such a person could be there on that occasion. Finally, when I heard this voice I always answered in my [native] Flemish language that this person should tell me where he was, that I would speak with him, and I asked him who he was. He never answered me, he only told me to leave that place. This never ceased to amaze me. What I imagine even today is that

---

8. See the glossary (*Raja Bongsu*).

it must have been one of the Dutchmen from among those who I had [earlier] met in the kingdom of Patani, who must have been aboard one of those ships, or an angel that was warning me, because I heard this voice [for] six or seven nights; not just once but on many occasions; not in one place but everywhere. I would hear it when I was walking downstream as well as when I was walking upstream, in such a manner that the voice put me on my guard and made me wary that some very great misfortune was about to befall me. Finally, on the orders of the king, they took my companion Júlio de Barros and me out from the prison. The king gave a letter to Júlio de Barros to take to the captain-major.[9] In the letter the king said that if [the captain-major] released the people from those two junks that he had seized, together with all their belongings and everything, then he would also release all the Christians whom he was holding prisoner along with their belongings; and that if [the captain-major] released the people from the junks without their belongings then he would do the same thing with the Christians.

[King 'Ala'uddin] dismissed me—since I did not have any properties—with another letter for the captain of Melaka [Fernão de Albuquerque]; and Khoja Ibrahim—that was the name of the ambassador—gave me another letter and told me to go in the company of the aforesaid two heathen merchants [Nina Aure and Nina Gadin]. I ordered my two slaves to be brought to me and I set out immediately without saying my farewells to those who were being held prisoner, because there was no more time to do anything. The following day at three o'clock in the afternoon I came near the estuary. I anchored off the coast of the city of Johor Lama and I came across Júlio de Barros, who was returning with the captain-major's reply and he was bringing an ailing Castilian with him. He told me to wait for him until the morning and that he would return in his junk, which was already loaded—and had been impounded by the king. I also came across a bantin from the fleet that had brought three Portuguese merchants from Melaka with their goods, to deliver them ashore. I warned them about what was happening and told them that they should not proceed to the

---

9.   Da Silva de Meneses.

city [of Batu Sawar] before gaining some information on what was going on there. Then one of the three merchants, seeing that the captain of the bantin did not wish to go to the city, persuaded his other two companions to disembark there at Johor Lama with their merchandise, saying that the king [of Johor] was a coward and that he would not dare to molest them. In effect, the captain of the bantin left all three of them along with their retainers and goods ashore. After they had disembarked the bantin moved away from the shore to return to the armada. At that very moment, I swear, the natives jumped on them and killed them, and seized their goods.

As soon as Júlio de Barros handed over Captain-Major [Da Silva de Meneses's] reply to the king [of Johor]—as was to be expected—the king immediately ordered that he be killed, along with all the Portuguese and Christians who were being held prisoner; in total they would have numbered some 150 persons. [The Johorese] had already tied Khoja Ibrahim's hands together in order to kill him. Since he was a Muslim [like them], however, the king spared his life. If I had been there I would undoubtedly have perished with all the others. When Júlio de Barros told me to wait for him I did not wish to do so. I sailed out of the river proffering heartfelt thanks to Our Lord, who, from among all the many people who were being held captive, saved just myself and the two Christian slaves of mine.

Another incident happened at the same time—after our armada had withdrawn to Melaka owing to the deaths that had taken place in Johor. In front of the Johor River the Dutch captured a carrack that was coming from China, which was importing more than two million in gold.[10] The owner of the carrack was Baltasar Serrão.[11] [The Dutch] captured some 500 Christian people along with this carrack—it was said that the king of Johor had informed

---

[10.] This is a reference to the seizure of the *Santa Catarina* off Singapore on 25 February 1603. See esp. SMS, pp. 68–75. The sum amounts to two million *cruzados* (of about 29 grams each) or the equivalent of 58 metric tons of coin-grade silver.

[11.] In other sources, including his letter to Van Heemskerck written after the seizure of the *Santa Catarina,* he signed his name as Sebastião (Sebastian). See SMS, pp. 75–7; and GPFT, p. 129. The confusion could have arisen based on the short-name "Bas" which can be a derivative of Sebastian or Balthasar.

Dutch pamphlet titled *Corte en sekere Beschrijvinge* (Short and Accurate Description) printed in Middelburg in 1604 in which the seizure of the *Santa Catarina* off Singapore in February 1603 is announced. The image depicts the three vessels of Jacob van Heemskerck attacking the Portuguese carrack while troops and some rowed vessels of the Johorese arrive at the scene of the naval engagement. The landscape and the city in the background are based on the artist's imagination. (Amsterdam University Library, OTM, Pfl. K. 26)

the Dutch how the fleet had withdrawn and that the carrack would have to pass through there—in order to take revenge on the Portuguese. I arrived in Melaka and handed over to the captain [of Melaka], Fernão de Albuquerque, the letters that the king of Johor had given me, along with the letters that ambassador [Khoja Ibrahim] had sent.

Memorials

How one can do
great damage to the Dutch

The first memorial, addressed to the Portuguese viceroy in Goa, explores the possibilities by which the Iberians could deal a serious blow to their Dutch competitors in Asia. In the opening lines, Jacques de Coutre urges the viceroy to relinquish the royal monopoly in pepper and permit private merchants to trade in this commodity. This memorial has led Juan José Morales and León Gómez Rivas to proclaim De Coutre an early champion of free trade.[1] The move to relinquish the royal monopoly and free-up commerce in the East Indies, heighten competition in commodities like pepper, and ultimately wipe out the profits of the Dutch, thus rendering their commercial activities in the East Indies unattractive. De Coutre furnishes an overview of geopolitics and trading opportunities around the Indian Ocean rim and the western Pacific, starting at the southern Cape of Good Hope, the eastern African coast, Arabia, Persia, India, Ceylon, Pegu, the Malay Peninsula, Sumatra, Borneo, Java and the Malukus, Siam, China and Japan. For each port or region, De Coutre describes the commodities or textiles that could be bought or sold. The following excerpts

---

[1]	Morales, J.J., review of "The Memoirs and Memorials of Jacques de Coutre", *Asian Review of Books,* 26 January 2014, http://www.asianreviewofbooks.com/new/?ID=1732. L. Gómez Rivas, "Quinientos años del descubrimiento del Pacífico", 29 January 2014, http://www.juandemariana.org/ comentario/6474/ quinientos/anos/descubrimiento/pacifico.

offer insights into the region around the Singapore Straits and the Johor River region.[2]

From Melaka the Portuguese used to go to Johor and to the kingdom of Pahang, and to the kingdom of Patani [situated] on the same coast, [and] to Ligor, Bordolong,[3] Siam, and to the city of Ayutthaya,[4] as well as to the kingdom of Cambodia. There was a Portuguese settlement there and monasteries with friars. The land used to belong to the king of Cambodia. The men from Melaka went to all these lands with their ships selling their textiles and other wares, and from there to Melaka they would bring a lot of gold and other wares, as I have mentioned, which were [then re-] shipped to India. The Portuguese from Melaka also went to Champa[5] and Cochinchina[6] and they took textiles and reals-of-eight, and coral. [On their return voyage] from there they had carracks laden with eaglewood, kalambak,[7] and benzoin.[8]

From Melaka carracks used to go to China, [specifically to] Macao, a Portuguese settlement in the land[s] of China. Many carracks from Goa also went to these lands and these carracks took to China many *pardaos*[9] of *reals* (which are reals-of-eight), *catechu*,[10]

---

2. Adapted from the summary in JDC, p. 49.
3. Port on the Isthmus of Kra. In early modern cartography it is often situated north of Kedah near two big swamps or estuaries. It is possible that it corresponds to Phatthalung in the south of present-day Thailand. See JDC, p. 354.
4. Royal administrative centre or capital of Siam (present-day Thailand).
5. A polity in the central southern coastal region of Indochina, present-day Vietnam. See JDC, pp. 356–7.
6. Name of a kingdom and also of a geographical name applied to the central regions of present-day Vietnam.
7. Highest-grade aloeswood, usually from Champa or the Malay Peninsula and Sumatra widely used in early modern Europe and Asia as medicine as well as in the production of incense. See JDC, pp. 325–6; SMS, p. 337.
8. A tree resin used in medicine as well as in the production of incense. See JDC, p. 306; SMS, p. 337.
9. An early modern Portuguese coin minted in gold or silver. In this instance the reference is to silver coins approximately the size of a real-of-eight. See JDC, pp. 333–4.
10. *Pucho* is the name in Melaka for *cate* or *catechu*. It was mixed with betel and areca for chewing. See JDC, pp. 302, 305, 306, 335–6.

coral, cat's eyes,[11] ambergris,[12] carnelian[13] from Cambay,[14] and wine and olive oil from Portugal. When they returned to Melaka they would pay duties to Your Majesty. If they went to Goa, these carracks would return richly laden with silk, and velvet fabrics, damask,[15] taffetas,[16] silk covers, and silk hangings to decorate homes, marquees, and gilded beds, and also many earrings, and Chinese porcelain, China root,[17] a lot of *tintinago*,[18] copper, a lot of alum stone,[19] *lengkuas*,[20] a lot of musk, gold, and rubies. Any of these carracks would import a million in gold.[21] They were large carracks and now not even small ships can navigate [these waters] because of the [Dutch] rebels.

From Melaka two or three carracks yearly went to Manila with textiles and many slaves, and from Manila to Melaka they would bring many reals-of-eight, and gold and cloves. From Melaka they also went to Borneo, which is a very large island, and from Melaka to Borneo they would take many textiles, as I have said. From there

---

[11.] A semi-precious stone.

[12.] See the glossary (*ambergris*).

[13.] A variant of the mineral chalcedony. In the early modern period it was commonly mounted in jewellery, carved into beads, or used in rosaries. See JDC, p. 313.

[14.] Port and city of the Gujarat sultanate and a major trading city. It was renowned for a number of goods such as cotton textiles. See JDC, p. 355.

[15.] A reversible fabric of cotton, silk or both. See JDC, p. 318.

[16.] A high-quality woven silk textile. See JDC, p. 345.

[17.] A knotty rhizome of the Sarsaparilla family and was widely procured as it found widespread application in the treatment of gout, skin disorders and to treat some symptoms of syphilis. See JDC, p. 336; SMS, p. 338; Borschberg, "The Euro-Asian Trade and Medicinal Usage of Radix Chinae", *Revista de Cultura*, International Edition 20 (2006): 102–15.

[18.] An alloy of copper and zinc and sometimes also lead. See JDC, pp. 346–7; SMS, p. 338.

[19.] A natural cosmetic containing potassium and alum crystal. Alum was used as an ingredient in dye to make the colour adhere to the cloth fibres. See JDC, p. 300.

[20.] A type of ginger or galangal. See JDC, p. 328.

[21.] This appears to be another term for a *conto de oro*, the equivalent of one million cruzados or the equivalent to about 29.1 metric tons of coin-grade silver. See JDC, p. 316.

they would bring back large quantities of camphor,[22] turtle [shells],[23] beeswax,[24] many slaves, bezoar stones, gold, and diamonds that are found on this island. This navigation has since ceased to exist on the Lawai River,[25] because the Dutch are continuously in the Strait of Singapore and [in] the Strait of Kundur, which [are] 30 [marine] *leguas*[26] from Melaka. All these carracks from Melaka that I have mentioned must perforce pass through these straits.

Two or three of Your Majesty's carracks also went to Melaka each year from Goa, and from there they went to the Malukus, to load cloves there on Your Majesty's behalf. From Melaka many Portuguese-owned ships went to Java, as well as [to] Palembang,[27] Sunda,[28] Arosbaya,[29] Banten,[30] Penarukan,[31] Pegu, Bima,[32] Solor,[33] [and] Timor.[34] From Melaka they took the wares I have mentioned, and from these places to Melaka they brought many spices and slaves. All these goods paid duties to Your Majesty. They used to go [on their outward and return journeys] through these said straits

---

22.　See the glossary (*camphor*).

23.　*Karet*, as turtle shell is known in Malay, was used for making certain personal luxury instruments (such as combs) or ornaments.

24.　Beeswax was widely used for making candles as well as in the design and preparation of traditional cloth wares in Southeast Asia, especially in the production of batik fabrics. See JDC, p. 305.

25.　See the list of place names (*Lawai*).

26.　Between about 165 and 180 kilometres.

27.　Port and polity located in central-eastern Sumatra. Though chiefly famous in the context of the pepper trade, Palembang was also a centre for eaglewood, beeswax and lakawood. See JDC, p. 374.

28.　Here presumably to the Strait of Sunda and the ports around it on Java and Sumatra.

29.　Port on north-western Madura Island. See JDC, p. 351.

30.　Port and polity in west Java near the Sunda Strait. See JDC, p. 352.

31.　Port and polity in northern Java near the Strait of Madura. See JDC, p. 373.

32.　Port city located on the western coast of the island of Sumbawa. Bima emerged a separate polity in the early 17th century after its ruler embraced Islam.

33.　An island of the eastern Indonesian Archipelago (*Nusa Tenggara*) located to the east of Flores and north of Timor. Acquired by the Portuguese in 1520, the island became an important post in the trade in sandalwood with Timor.

34.　An island in the eastern region of the Indonesian Archipelago. Timor was an important region linked to the trade in white sandalwood and beeswax. See JDC, p. 383.

where the Dutch are now continually present. As they have their fortresses close by there, such as [the] city of Ambon,[35] which used to belong to the Portuguese. [There is also] Jayakerta[36] and other Dutch fortresses and factories such as Johor, Patani, Ayutthaya, Lawai, Sukadana,[37] and Banjarmasin,[38] Makassar, and the Malukus.[39] The Dutch have taken all these harbours; it is very worrying.

From Melaka they went to Sumatra, which is across [the strait] from Melaka. They went with textiles to Siak and Kampar,[40] and they brought from there a lot of gold, and porcupine bezoars, and many provisions. The local people are [called] Minangkabau. From Melaka they also went to Aceh with textiles, silk pieces, eaglewood, and a lot of golden thread. It is a large port. Many Dutch carracks go there to load pepper, as do Turkish carracks and carracks from Aden,[41] Masulipatam,[42] and Pegu. But these Acehnese are very treacherous: they are bad people, you cannot trust them nor any blacks from the South.[43] It is necessary to be very careful when dealing with them.

[35.] Island and port city located in the Malukus, and a trading post of importance for the spice trade (cloves, nutmeg, mace). The town of Ambon traces its origin to a settlement located outside the walls of the late 16th century Portuguese fortress. The town and fort of Ambon fell to the Dutch in 1605. See also JDC, p. 251.

[36.] See the list of place names (*Jayakerta*).

[37.] River, port and polity on the island of Borneo in the present-day State of Sarawak, Malaysia. Sukadana was most famous for its diamonds. See JDC, pp. 380–1.

[38.] A kingdom in the south of Borneo around the Barito River. Its capital was a noteworthy source of rattan, lakawood, beeswax, gold dust, precious stones (especially diamonds), bezoars and dragon's blood. See JDC, p. 362.

[39.] See the list of place names (*Maluku*).

[40.] River, port and polity in central-eastern Sumatra. In the early modern period Kampar was important for pepper trade and also as a source of gold dust. See JDC, p. 355.

[41.] Leading port city located of the southern coast of the Arabian Peninsula in present-day Yemen. See JDC, p. 250.

[42.] Port on the south-eastern (Coromandel) coast of India. Masulipatam maintained close trading connections in textiles with Bengal and was known for its cloth pieces and finished clothing. See JDC, p. 370.

[43.] From Southeast Asia. See also the list of place names (*South*).

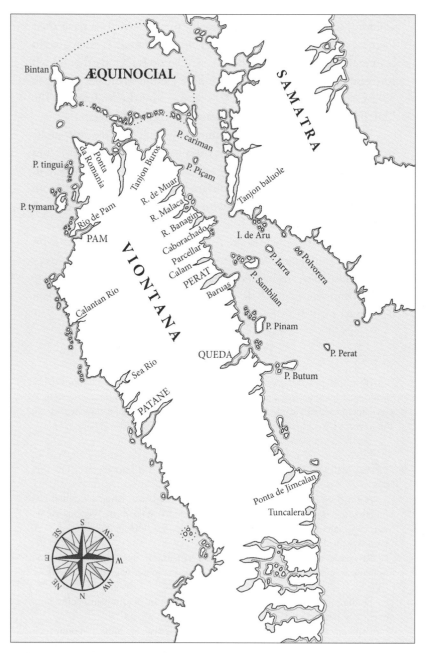

Redrawn map of the Malay Peninsula by Manoel Godinho de Erédia, c. 1613. This map corresponds to a sample found in his *Description of Melaka*.

On the coast of Sumatra there are also two rivers or ports; one is called Jambi[44] and the other Indragiri.[45] These lands have a lot of pepper and the settlements are along the rivers. Many ships from Patani, known as junks, go inside these lands to load pepper on behalf of the Dutch. The city of Patani is on the same coast of Melaka,[46] some 150 [marine] *leguas*[47] outside the Strait of Singapore. There are two Dutch factories in this land of Patani. There the [Dutch] carracks load this pepper from Jambi and Indragiri, and from Aceh, and this is the pepper that they take to Holland. No peppercorns are taken from India. They buy this pepper in exchange for pieces of crimson textile and other fabrics from Europe, barrel guns, and other small items, as well as reals-of-eight.

[44.] River, polity and settlement located in central-eastern Sumatra. Jambi was second to Aceh as a trading centre for pepper during the late 16th and early 17th centuries. See JDC, p. 364.

[45.] River, port and polity located in central-eastern Sumatra. Indragiri was an important port in the early modern pepper trade. See JDC, p. 351.

[46.] In this instance the toponym "Malacca" almost certainly refers to the whole western coast of the Malay Peninsula. See also the list of place names (*Melaka*).

[47.] Between about 825 and 925 kilometres.

Information about building some castles and fortresses in the Straits of Singapore and other regions of the South, etc.

In this memorial, Jacques de Coutre delves into the issues of geopolitics and security. From the opening lines of his piece it is clear that the measures he is recommending are targeted at the Dutch who were seriously disrupting Portuguese trade across the region. He lists a number of places connected by the network centred at Melaka: Johor, Pahang, Patani, Ligor, Siam, Cambodia, Champa, Cochinchina, China, Manila, Japan, Borneo and the Ryukyu Islands and of course other ports along the Malay Coast, across the Bay of Bengal and beyond. To successfully revive and also secure seaborne trade for the Portuguese, he recommends stepping up security at a crucial nodal point in this eastern section of the trade network: the Singapore Straits. To achieve this end, it would be highly advisable to construct a series of fortifications, starting with three on and around Singapore Island. This memorial advises in detail what the viceroy should do, and where he should build the proposed fortifications.

The coast of Melaka extends north and south nearly as far as the Strait of Singapore.[1] Many ships go to Melaka and return through this strait. [These are] large and small *baxels* from

---

[1]   See the list of place names (*New / Old Strait of Singapore*).

the following kingdoms: Johor, Pahang, Patani, Ligor,[2] Siam, Cambodia, Champa, Cochinchina, and carracks and junks from China, Zhangzhou, Manila, Japan, and some baxels from the Malukus, and from the kingdoms of Borneo, Lawai, Banjarmasin, and from all the islands of Borneo. All these vessels pass through this Strait of Singapore.

When the Javanese come to know that in Melaka there is some captain who mistreats them—as sometimes has been the case—though their course is through the Strait of Kundur to Melaka, they go from inside and around the islands in search of the island of Bintan, and they go to Johor. These vessels come laden with nutmeg, mace, cloves and other merchandise. The Portuguese then go from Melaka to Johor with cloth to sell, they buy spices and other commodities and [then] return to Melaka. All these vessels and wares pass through these Straits of Singapore.

All this commerce described above has been usurped by the rebels. They are the ones who today benefit from this trade. To remedy this state of affairs and redirect trade to Melaka, Your Majesty must order that a very strong fortress or citadel be built in the Straits of Singapore, with a good garrison and good artillery, munitions and supplies as is advisable. The residents of the citadel could also acquire supplies from the vessels that pass through these straits, both from those that sail towards Melaka as well as those that are going to Aceh; on their outward as well as on their return journey.

In the middle of the Singapore Straits there is an island,[3] which measures more or less three *leguas*.[4] The Old Strait is [situated] on one side of that island, the New Strait on the other. This island forms a rocky point [which is located] between the [two] Straits [and] that resembles a fortress created by nature. This point is called *Surgídera*;[5] the Old Strait lies on one side [of it], and the New Strait

---

2. Port and polity situated on the Isthmus of Kra along the Gulf of Siam. The town of Ligor is present-day Nakhon Si Thammarat in Thailand.
3. This is a reference to present-day Sentosa.
4. About six kilometres.
5. In this instance *Surgídera* means a place or point of anchorage. See also the list of place names (*Surgídera*).

on the other. Your Majesty should order that a very strong citadel be built on this peak. All the vessels that pass through these Straits, through the Old Strait as well as through the New Strait, stop and drop anchor around this point. It is necessary to do so because two [daily] tides pass through these Straits, entering from one side as well as from the other.

The Old Strait is so narrow that it can be closed off with a chain. The New Strait is wider, but no vessel can pass through either of these straits without being within reach of the citadel, which can sink them with its artillery. At [*Surgídera*] point [the water] is 14 *brazas* deep.[6] As one comes from Melaka [one passes] the promontory of Tanjung Bulus,[7] and enters this Strait of Singapore between the Ilha das Cobras[8] and another island that is densely forested with trees that they call *salgeros*.[9] Entering by the middle [the water measures] eight *brazas*[10] deep; when approaching the aforementioned [*Surgídera*] point 10 and 12 *brazas,* and 14 next to it.[11] [Passing] through the Old Strait from this point [the water measures] eight, seven and six [*brazas*] up to the exit;[12] [passing through] the New Strait from [*Surgídera*] point the water measures twelve, ten and eight *brazas* until one exits.[13]

One can drop anchor anywhere in these straits since these channels are safely sheltered from storms, as though one were in a river. This is because there are strong currents. Ships with three and four decks can pass through these straits, such as the carracks from

---

[6.]   A unit for measuring the depth of water; here about 23.4 metres. See also JDC, pp. 308–9.

[7.]   The southernmost tip of Peninsular Malaysia, located in the State of Johor due west of present-day Singapore. See JDC, p. 382.

[8.]   Literally "Island of the Cobras"; present-day Pulau Merambong. Judging by the maps of Erédia, the old Malay name appears to have been Pulau Ular (Snake Island). See JDC, p. 385 as well as the maps on pp. 18, 30, 33, 81.

[9.]   This appears to be a reference to the western side of present-day Singapore Island.

[10.]   About 13.4 metres.

[11.]   About 16.7, 20 and 23.4 metres.

[12.]   About 13.4, 11.7 and 10 metres.

[13.]   About 20, 16.7 and 13.4 metres.

Portugal. At the tip of this island[14] the *baxels* can come so close to shore that it is possible to disembark on a plank if necessary. The island is very lush with trees with [thick] foliage, and it [also] has very good [fresh] water. This is why Your Majesty should order a fort or citadel to be built on this island, as mentioned above. This island has a number of stone cliffs, [where] it is not easy to disembark, but it is none the worse for this. There are some salgeros beside this point.

On the side of the New Strait, one could build a quay there for *batels* and galleys, [and] ships, as well as to service this citadel. The island has places that are flat, and others with cliffs. When our ships come and go to China and the Manilas[15] and other parts, they—and other friendly *baxels*—can take shelter below the citadel when they hear news of enemies [approaching]. There are many fishermen called *saletes*[16] who live in these Straits. They are local people, Malays. If one accompanies and pays them, they will serve that person well. These people visit all the islands around these Straits, and when there are enemies, they come to warn [us] in exchange for [a piece of] cloth worth four *reals*[17] (which they are given) and for them to remain under our protection.

For the purpose of [maintaining] this commerce, Your Majesty must maintain in the [Singapore] Straits five or six well-armed Manila galleys, [that be] placed under [the command of] the citadel to patrol the straits. These Manila galleys are sufficiently light that they can enter and leave with ease whenever necessary. The enemy will [then] not be in a position to capture as many [vessels] as they now habitually do, nor given the presence of the galleys will they be able to keep one ship at one entrance of the strait and another at the opposite entrance, as they generally do now, and capture all the junks that pass through these straits. The enemy will no longer be able to separate their ships from one another because of the lulls and the absence of wind that prevails in this region. This

---

14. At the location of Fort Siloso on Sentosa.
15. This toponym is to be understood here as the Philippines in general.
16. That is *orang laut*. See also the glossary (*orang laut*).
17. About 15.5 grams of coin-grade silver.

way the [galleys] can patrol the straits, and the vessels mentioned earlier would be able to call at this fort and [also] at Melaka. This is presently not possible because the enemy impedes them from doing so. These galleys can proceed to the Strait of Kundur. From there one [strait] is no more than ten [marine] *leguas*[18] away from the other, and there are many channels for the galleys to pass through the said Strait of Kundur. Thus, in a few days they will know all the passageways owing to the fishermen who are known as *orang laut*. These *orang laut* live aboard very small vessels. They sleep there and live and are born on their boats. In short, these vessels are their home.

When our armada arrives at this place to build this citadel, it will then be necessary to entrench oneself at the aforementioned [*Surgídera*] point with sacks of earth,[19] and place the artillery in the middle according to the manner and design of the citadel to be built. There is no lack of wood there to entrench oneself while one prepares materials to build the fortification. There is no lack of stone there either and [there are] lots of white stones from the sea called [*batu*] *karang*,[20] which are like limestone or gypsum. There is also a lot of firewood to burn after having made provisions for materials. [The men of the armada] will then be able to begin constructing the walls and the bulwarks and whatever else is advisable. When they finish a bulwark they can begin to build another, so that they are always entrenched [and prepared] for anything unforeseen. For this and other purposes Your Majesty must dispatch engineers who are well versed in [building] fortifications.

It is advisable that these [proposed] citadels be impregnable, [for] then the rebels will not be able to pass through here, nor the [king of] Aceh with his armadas to sack Johor or the kingdom of Pahang. They would be forced to pass through the Strait of Kundur and bypass the islands, or sail between them. [In any case] it would significantly constrain [their movements]. When we have galleys stationed there, they can patrol the Strait of Kundur. Although

---

18. About 55 to 62 kilometres.
19. It is assumed De Coutre actually means sacks of rock or sand in this instance.
20. This is the Malay word for coral. It was pounded up and used as mortar.

this strait is broad, it features a lot of shoals. Sometimes carracks remain [here] seven or eight days without being able to sail through because of contrary winds, even when the tide is in their favour. It is a challenging strait, and the galleys are thus ideally suited for capturing ships lying at anchor. In this way the [galleys] will inflict a great deal of damage on the enemy.

The rebels come with their ships to load pepper, drop anchor and moor around the said Strait of Kundur outside the Indragiri and Jambi Rivers, where [the water] is not very deep. No more than about 25 [marine] *leguas*[21] separate the aforementioned point from these river estuaries. Meanwhile, our galleys can be on [their heels] night or day, and our enemies will not be able to load pepper, which is the mainstay of their commerce [in the East Indies].[22] Since it [would be] close to our [proposed] fortress, our men would be able to trade and negotiate. Only small vessels enter this river.[23] Nor would the rebels find refuge in Palembang, which is a kingdom that has always been on friendly terms with [the Portuguese].[24] So, with these galleys and the citadel one could inflict a great [deal of] damage to the enemy and his trade, and [also] be able to patrol the straits. When these straits are patrolled and free [of enemy craft], all the vessels will come from all around to call at the fort and [also] Melaka, because the *Indios*[25] prefer to sell their wares to us, rather than to the [Dutch] rebels, because the rebels charge levies on all their merchandise, both on what they buy as well as what they sell. [The *Indios*] evidently do not like the [Dutch] rebels, because they do not sell nor buy like the Portuguese used to do.

---

21. Between about 138 and 150 kilometres.
22. Admiral Matelieff reported for the early period of the VOC in question here that over half of total cargo value brought back to the Dutch Republic was in pepper. See CMJ, p. 218.
23. Perhaps De Coutre implies only one or both the Jambi and Indragiri Rivers.
24. To the Portuguese.
25. This is a generic term applied to all the peoples in India and eastwards, including the Malay Archipelago and the Philippines.

It is necessary to build a second fortress or citadel in the Johor River estuary at the promontory[26] of the *Isla de la Sabandaría Vieja*.[27] This island is situated in the Johor River estuary and is bordered by the Old Strait and Teberau Strait. This [second] fortress should be located about three [marine] *leguas*[28] from the [first fortress located] at the [Singapore] Straits.[29] This *Isla de la Sabandaría Vieja* measures about seven [marine] *leguas* across.[30] The [second] citadel situated at the Johor River estuary and the [first one] at the Singapore Straits can lend each other assistance either by sea or by land. The Old Strait is situated between one island and the other.[31] It resembles a river that can be sealed off with a chain. At this [second] location Your Majesty must order a citadel to be built like the first one that has been mentioned [above]. [Your Majesty] should become the lord of this port, which is one of the best that serves the [East] Indies. [Your Majesty] can build a city there and become the lord of this kingdom. By constructing this citadel there, no enemy ships would be able to enter without being sunk, even though the Johor River is wide and near the promontory at Johor Lama there is a shoal [completely] surrounded by sea.[32]

---

26. A reference to present-day Changi Point, also known from 17th century Portuguese cartographical specimens (esp. Manuel Godinho de Erédia) as Tanjung Rusa (sometimes spelled *Ruça*).

27. Singapore Island. See also the glossary (*Sabandaria*).

28. Between about 16 to 18 kilometres.

29. The current site of Fort Siloso.

30. Between about 39 and 44 kilometres.

31. Between the main island of Singapore and present-day Sentosa.

32. The location of this shoal is not certain. There is indeed a promontory located to the south of Johor Lama. The promontory in question is almost certainly located to the south of the recently completed bridge across the Johor River (E22) connecting the road between Senai and Desaru. Another possible location would be located to the south of the bridge around Pulau Tekong Besar (Pula Chagni on the maps of Erédia) from where it would have been possible to monitor waterborne traffic entering the main branch of the river, or alternatively through one of the two branches of the Teberau Strait separated by Pulau Ubin.

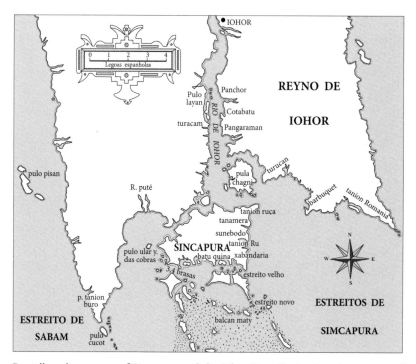

Partially redrawn map of Singapore and the Johor River Region based on a map of 1615 contained in the *Atlas Miscelânea,* fol. 41 recto, ascribed to Manuel Godinho de Erédia, and titled "Taboa dos Estreitos de Sabam e de Sincapura com o Rio de Ihor" (Map of the Straits of Kundur and Singapore with the Johor River). In the 1960s, the original belonged to the private collection of Dr. C.M.C. Machado Figueiro of Lisbon. The current whereabouts of the *Atlas* is unknown. A photograph of the map was reproduced in the *Portugaliae Monumenta Cartographica* of Armando Cortesão and Avelino Teixeira de Mota, vol. IV, plate 417B.

When large ships arrive, they move closer to the point where the fortress should be built, and across, [just] a stone's throw away, the [aforementioned] shoal [is located]. A small fort could be built on that shoal to monitor the entire [Johor] River and to prevent both large and small *baxels* from entering. The enemy rebels repair and careen their ships in this river estuary. The [Johor] River is very wide and beautiful; ships laden with wares can enter and exit without any danger up to 10 or even 12 *leguas* upstream.[33] There is no lack of wood in these parts to entrench oneself after arriving, nor is there a lack of materials [with which] to build the citadel, nor a dearth of stones with which to make lime and plaster. In this port,[34] near the aforesaid promontory,[35] the Portuguese captured—[or should one better say] Dom Paulo de Lima[36] captured—Johor Lama, but they did not wish to keep it.

The king of the city of Johor Lama fled and went to live on the island of Bintan, and later returned and built another city, [located] 14 [marine] *leguas* upstream, which is called Batu Sawar, [but which] the Portuguese call "New Johor". The king of Aceh[37] captured this port and has kept it occupied. But it could be taken with 1,500 men, as could the city of Pahang, which this king of Aceh has [also] occupied. For this purpose it would be good to call on the aforementioned king of Johor, since there are four brothers,[38] and put one of them in power. Once we have constructed the citadels, we will be safe from the people of the land, and Your Majesty would

---

33. Between about 55 to 70 kilometres.
34. The port of Johor Lama.
35. Two promontories have been mentiond by De Coutre, one to the south of Johor Lama, or the one at Changi Point (Tanjung Rusa).
36. Dom Paulo de Lima Pereira launched an attack on Johor Lama and the fortress Kota Batu in the year 1587. See SMS, esp. pp. 209–28.
37. Iskandar Muda of Aceh. The Acehnese launched a successful attack on the Johor River region and Batu Sawar in 1613. See SMS, pp. 112–5.
38. These four brothers are: Ala'uddin Ri'ayat Shah who ruled as sultan between 1597–1613/15; Raja Bongsu, later Sultan Ma'ayat Shah, who ruled from 1613/15–23, as well as the Raja Laut and Raja Siak. For a contemporaneous description of them by Dutch Admiral Cornelis Matelieff de Jonge from 1606, see CMJ, pp. 153-4, as well as GPFT, appendix 13, pp. 211–3.

have a vassal king [just] like the king of Hormuz[39] used to be. When the natives will see their monarch and our protection, all of them will rise up against the [king of] Aceh on the island of Sumatra, Siak,[40] Kampar, Bengkalis and the lands of Aru,[41] for they are Malays.[42]

This land used to belong to the king of Johor, and the island of Sumatra features a kingdom that was governed by Raja Siak, who was a brother of this king of Johor.[43] Siak is situated at the entrance of the Kundur Strait, [and the *raja*] controlled more than 60 *leguas*[44] of coastline. The king of Aceh has now occupied all of it. Your Majesty could maintain galleys and galleons[45] in this Johor River. They can enter and exit with the tide and wind. If Your Majesty had six or seven Dunkirk galleons in this port,[46] the rebels would not be safe anywhere in the South, because the [Dutch] rebels drop anchor and moor more than a *legua* and a half[47] [from the shore] in each and every port in the South. It is possible to get close to them, because they are separated from one another—there is one ship in one port, two in another. As has been said, with the help of the fishermen,[48] our ships can glean information on the whereabouts of the [Dutch] rebels and attack them. As they belong to a single people, our men are very often mistaken for the [Dutch] rebels, both by night and by day. In this way one can deprive the rebels of commerce and destroy them.

[39.] Port located in the south of present-day Iran near the entrance to the Persian Gulf. Hormuz was ruled by a king who was subservient to the Portuguese between 1507 and 1620. The English took the city in 1622. See JDC, p. 372.

[40.] A river and polity located in central-eastern Sumatra. Siak is historically associated with Johor in the early 17th century. See JDC, pp. 279–80.

[41.] See the list of place names (*Aru*).

[42.] Here De Coutre intimates that while the peoples of Siak, Kampar, Bengkalis and Aru (all locations on Sumatra) were considered "Malays", the Acehnese who were their overlords were not.

[43.] For the identity of Raja Siak, see the glossary (*Raja Siak*).

[44.] About 330 to 360 kilometres.

[45.] An ocean-going ship developed after the late 16th century and improved in size and design over almost two centuries. They could act as a vessel of burden or a navy ship. See also JDC, p. 322–3; SMS, pp. 332–3.

[46.] The port in question here is probably *Sabandaría* (Singapore).

[47.] About eight to nine kilometres.

[48.] The *orang laut*.

In order to construct these fortifications, it will be necessary that Your Majesty dispatch 20 galleons with Castilian Spaniards,[49] among them [should be] about six or seven Dunkirk galleons, which make a total of 20 galleons. [They need to be] well-equipped with artillery and supplies, with each having 250 men, and some engineers with the appropriate tools [to build] the fortifications. On arriving in the Strait of Singapore they can inform Manila, [and] should there be an armada [stationed] there it could come and join them. [In Manila there are] principally the galleys. Your Majesty must dispatch skilled craftsmen to the Johor River who know how to build galleys. There is no lack of [construction] sites or wood to build them, there is [also] no lack of trees to make masts for the galleys, nor [a lack of] cordage, ribs, oars, pitch, [or] oil with which to paint the hull.

As for the crews for the galleys, *kaffirs*[50] can be brought from Goa. They are strong, dark-skinned people like those from Angola. They can be bought in Goa for 20 reals-of-eight[51] per head. From Manila the Spanish go to Goa to buy [them] for their galleys, and they load ships [full] of these people. Our ships could also proceed to the Coromandel Coast and load textiles and take on spices like the Dutch do. Your Majesty has two ports on the Coromandel Coast, one is called Nagapattinam[52] and the other São Tomé,[53] where one could dispose of these cargoes. The Portuguese profit greatly from this commerce. From Johor or from the Strait [of Singapore] one can send ships laden with spices to Spain like the Portuguese do, and in this way one will fill Spain, Castile and Portugal with spices,

---

49. Spaniards from Castile.

50. Term of Arabic origin used to designate a person who is not a Muslim. The Spanish and the Portuguese adopted this expression during the early modern period and often employed it as a pejorative. It generically refers to persons of colour, including especially Africans and south Indians.

51. About 600 grams of coin-grade silver.

52. A port located on the Coromandel Coast and effectively controlled by the Portuguese. In the early 17th century it exported cotton pieces to Southeast Asia. See JDC, p. 371.

53. See the list of place names (*Mylapur*).

and Your Majesty's customs houses will yield much more. From there[54] merchants can send [these wares] to France and Germany.

In this way, the Dutch will not be able to make such profits, and consequently they and their trade will diminish. As [the VOC] is a company of merchants [and] if there are no profits, each one will withdraw from this company, in view of low profits. Manila and these two citadels or fortresses, [together with] Melaka and Macao, can assist one another, because they are not a great distance away from each other. [As for] the two citadels, one in the Straits and the other at the mouth of the Johor River,[55] it is necessary that they both be built in a trice. This will enable them to assist and help one another by sea and by land, as has been mentioned above. It will be necessary to entrench oneself quickly: there is no absence of safe locations, nor will there be anyone [there] to [stop] them. Before the [Dutch] rebels learn about [the arrival of our men], they will already have established themselves. [Your Majesty] can station ten galleons in the Straits by the fortress and another ten at the mouth of the Johor River, until these citadels have been secured. After constructing the two citadels, [Your Majesty] can build [yet another one] in the Muar River estuary;[56] then the king of Aceh will not be able to assist Johor in any way, neither by sea nor by land.

[The Muar] River is very beautiful and much better than the Melaka River. One can enter the Muar River with junks, *balas*, *lancharas*[57]—which are vessels of the people of the land—or [also] laden galliots.[58] [Large] ships cannot enter [the river], but they can drop anchor and moor close by as they do in Melaka. It has a good site to harbour galleys and foists,[59] and there is also no lack of secure

---

54. The Iberian Peninsula.
55. At Changi Point.
56. A similar proposal on the identical site was also mooted (and drawn) by De Coutre's contemporary Erédia in his *Description of Malaca*. See the image in SMS, p. 57.
57. These terms refer to small Asian vessels that were propelled by breast oars and could also be sailed. See also JDC, pp. 305, 327; SMS, p. 333.
58. A type of vessel featuring one or two masts and a shallow draft. The galliot could be sailed or propelled by breast oars. See also JDC, p. 323; SMS, p. 333.
59. A type of vessel that normally featured a single row of oars and a single mast. See JDC, p. 321; SMS, p. 332.

places to construct [such vessels]. [Your Majesty] can build this fortress without hindrance from the natives. There is a very small village nearby. It is not very noteworthy—it is called Muar—but it has a very beautiful beach that is two *leguas* long.[60] Next to this beach there are some huts of minor significance; they belong to fishermen. Afterwards, these people will obey us and will come to live around our fort, and consequently also the people of Johor.

In the aforementioned city of Johor,[61] there are many people who make a living only from merchandise and [from] sailing from one land to another.

This is the best way to destroy and diminish the [Dutch] rebels as per my understanding in good faith. If Your Majesty were to send 40 galleons, it would be more effective to put an end to, destroy, and expel the Dutch who are in the East Indies.

Jacques de Coutre devised this plan of the site of the Straits of Singapore and Kundur. To remedy these regions he gives to Your Excellency this information according to what appears [to be] and [as] discussed with Your Excellency in the past days, especially about depriving the Dutch of the commerce that they have in the East Indies, etc.

Jaques de Couttre

Information that Jacques de Coutre sends to Your Highness to construct forts in the Straits of Singapore and in the Johor River estuary in the East Indies, etc.

---

60. Here probably about four kilometres.
61. Batu Sawar.

Information for Your Majesty to remedy the Estado da Índia

This memorial, which is divided into two main sections, walks the reader through two scenarios in which Jacques de Coutre argues it would be possible to reverse the declining fortunes of the *Estado da Índia*. The first scenario involves large-scale naval intervention against the Dutch similar to the joint Luso-Spanish intervention in Brazil in the year 1625. The second section assumes that large-scale naval intervention against the Dutch is not possible. This scenario involves sending annually a fleet of smaller ships (preferably caravels)[1] to the East Indies to reduce the risk of loss when captured. These vessels would engage both in trade as well as in raiding. Additional measures are then recommended for upgrading fortifications in the *Estado da Índia*, singling out Goa for discussion. The following excerpt taken from this memorial identify and briefly discuss the nature of the trading networks focused in and around Melaka and the Straits as well as the possibility of securing Portuguese interests in the region.

Part II

Your Majesty should order that four or five Spanish galleys—there are very good galleys there—go from Manila to Melaka so that they can be used to capture enemy carracks, since the coast of Melaka is calmer than that of the aforementioned [city of] Manila.[2]

---

1. A sailing ship with a shallow draft and two or three masts with lateen (triangular) sails favoured by the Spaniards in the early phase of the explorations. See JDC, p. 312.
2. De Coutre means the waters of the Melaka Strait are comparatively calmer

They would capture some enemy carracks in the Strait of Singapore and in the Strait of Kundur, and they could watch over those straits, and it would send a strong message to the enemy. [The Dutch] ships would not sail so far apart. They would be obliged to sail together owing to the periods when there are no winds, when they are vulnerable, and the galleys could easily capture them. When their ships sail together they will not be able to capture that many prizes and they will not be able to be at all the entrances of the straits as they are now. Now, only very few vessels escape capture by them. When the aforementioned straits are free, ships can come from China, the coast of Patani, and Java to Melaka. Your Majesty's customs and excise houses would generate far more revenues. Galleys can also be made in Melaka too, if there were master ship builders who could design and construct them, because there is no dearth of carpenters there and there is also very good timber for the rigging and planks for the oars. There is no shortage of men there to serve as crews on the galleys, who are dark like the inhabitants of Angola;[3] they are called *kaffirs*. They can be bought cheaply in India and are good as crews for galleys. In Manila the Spanish value them highly and treat them very well; so much so that these Spaniards go from Manila to Goa to buy these slaves for the galleys and they bring back shiploads of them.

With regard to the Straits of Singapore, between these straits there is an island.[4] The New Strait is on one side of this island and the Old Strait is on the other. The island is triangular and all the ships and vessels that pass through these two straits first anchor a stone's throw away from land. Your Majesty should order that a castle or fortress be built on this island, [equipped] with good pieces of artillery. One would then be able to monitor these two [Singapore] Straits, and no ship or vessel would be able to pass through the straits that could not be sunk. The [north-western] tip of this island is a natural fortification and its tip is made up of rock. This fortress could be built at little cost. The island has a cooling

---

than the open seas around the coast of Luzon where Manila is located.

3. From the coastal regions of central south-western Africa.
4. Present-day Sentosa.

climate surrounded by leafy trees and it has excellent [fresh] water. This fortress would be very useful and could serve as a safe refuge for ships from China, both on the outward as well as on the return voyage. If our ships are under the fortress, they will be safe.

They could have bantins (which are some vessels that they use there) to go through these straits and keep an eye on the whereabouts of the enemy. [The bantins] can [then] warn our ships coming or going to China, and inform them through which strait they can sail safely without fearing the enemy. These vessels are like *brigantines*;[5] they call them bantins, as said. They also serve to tow ships and guide ships through the entrances of these straits,[6] remove them from some shoals, or also to tow vessels to escape from the enemy, and for many other things. Your Majesty should order that they do not sail except with oared galliots, as aforesaid. In this manner there will be trade and Your Majesty's customs houses will generate revenue (even though it will not be as it used to be in the past) and sustain the lands. When the merchants will be able to sail freely, without the hindrance of the captains of the *viagens*,[7] they will be encouraged to face the risks of going to sea and build ships.

Your Majesty should order that the lands of Melaka[8]—very good and very verdant lands—are settled with people that are called *Chincheos*[9] there, just like the Spanish have in Manila.[10] These men are very agile and hardworking and cultivate the land, or raise oxen and cows, pigs and chickens, all of which are in short supply. They are great fishermen and expert at all kinds of crafts:

---

5. A small sailing vessel that can also be propelled by breast oars and usually featuring one or two masts. De Coutre claimed they are similar to bantins. See JDC, p. 309.

6. The Straits of Singapore.

7. Concession voyages. See also the glossary (*viagem*).

8. From the context that follows this is a reference to the lands immediately surrounding the city of Melaka, rather than the whole of the Malay Peninsula which in European cartography was also commonly referred to as *Malacca* during the early modern period.

9. The name commonly employed by the Portuguese and especially the Spanish to generically refer to people from China, and specifically from the coastal region of Fujian (Amoy Coast). See JDC, pp. 315, 357.

10. See De Coutre's brief discussion of the Chinese of Manila in JDC, pp. 155–6.

carpenters, bricklayers, blacksmiths, and all the professions that are needed in a city. They should send for other people from their land to populate these lands of Melaka, which are entirely surrounded by forests and have no inhabitants, except for a few poor people who live under the walls of this city of Melaka, [as well as those] who live on the outskirts.

To inform Your Majesty about the commerce that used to take place in India: First from the South: some years ago more than 500 vessels, large and small, *viz.* ships, junks, *balas, lancharas*, would frequent the harbour or port of Melaka, a fortress that belongs to Your Majesty, and all these vessels would bring wares to trade. The junks that arrived from the islands of Banda[11] and from Makassar, and from the island of Java and from all [nearby] kingdoms, came laden with mace, nutmeg, and cloves, benzoin, sugar, rattan, [12] beeswax, and other wares. Other junks that came from the kingdom of Borneo came laden with [sea] turtle shell, camphor,[13] and beeswax, and they brought many bezoar stones, some diamonds, and gold.[14] Other junks came from the kingdoms of Johor, Pahang, Patani, Ligor,[15] and Siam. These junks brought sappan[wood][16] [that is used] to make dyes to colour [the] textiles that are produced on the Coromandel Coast,[17] They brought civet,[18] beeswax, and large quantities of very

---

[11.] Island group located to the south of the Malukus. The Bandas, including its main island Lontor (Great Banda), was renowned for the cultivation of nutmeg and its by-product mace. Banda was taken by the Dutch in 1609.

[12.] A strong cane-like vine harvested across Southeast Asia from the creeping stems of a climbing palm. Rattan is more pliable than bamboo and could be split and twisted to make thick cables for ships or woven into sails for junks. See JDC, p. 338.

[13.] See the glossary (*camphor*).

[14.] See De Coutre's account of Brunei in JDC, pp. 147–8.

[15.] Present-day Nakhon Si Thammarat.

[16.] A prized tree native to Southeast Asia used for extracting a red-coloured dye and also as a medicinal substance. It was and still is often compared to brazilwood. See JDC, p. 341.

[17.] The south-eastern coast of subcontinental India, approximately equivalent to the coastal regions of the Indian State of Tamil Nadu.

[18.] A word of Arabic origin referring to the odoriferous excretion of the so-called "civet cat". The civet cat, however, is not a feline but a relative of the bear. See JDC p. 316.

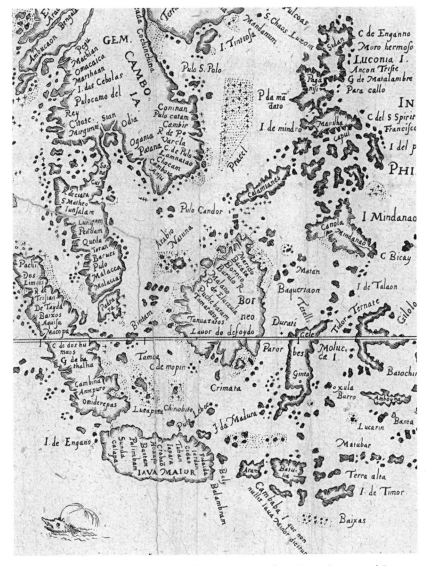

Section of a printed map of Asia by Theodore de Bry from Isaac Genius and Levinus Hulsius, *Neundte Schiffart* (Ninth Dutch Voyage to the East Indies) printed in Frankfurt am Main in 1612. (The Hague, National Library of the Netherlands, 2112 C 4)

good benzoin, and a lot of gold to buy textiles. Other junks arrived from the kingdoms of Cambodia, Champa, and Cochinchina. These junks came laden with eaglewood, kalambak, and benzoin, and they brought a lot of gold. All [of this] was exchanged for textiles. Other junks arrived from the kingdoms of Jambi, Indragiri, Siak, Kampar, Perak,[19] and Kedah.[20] These junks brought pepper, tin and gold to exchange for textiles.

Furthermore, 35 or 40 ships used to come to Melaka from Goa, Chaul,[21] Cochin,[22] Nagapattinam, Mylapur,[23] from all [along] the Coromandel Coast, from the kingdoms of Bengal,[24] as well as Pegu. All these ships came laden with textiles from Cambay and Sindh, and other textiles from the Coromandel Coast. [Still more] ships [came] laden with textiles, and *colchas*,[25] and very beautiful marquees that can be assembled. From the kingdoms of Bengal and Pegu they brought a lot of lac,[26] beeswax, provisions, and many precious stones such as rubies and sapphires. From Goa and other lands the ships brought a lot of wheat, wine, olive oil and butter. The city of Melaka does not have any of this. Likewise four more

---

[19.]   River, port and polity situated in the central-western region of the Malay Peninsula. Perak was chiefly known in the early modern period as a supplier of tin.

[20.]   River, port, settlement and polity in the north-western regions of the Malay Peninsula important in the context of the pepper and tin trade. In the 16th and 17th centuries, the Portuguese regarded Kedah as a vassal or client state of Siam. It was attacked and overrun by Aceh in 1619.

[21.]   Port and city located on the western coast of India. Originally ruled by the sultan of Gujarat, Chaul was taken over by the Portuguese in 1521 where they ruled until 1740. See JDC, p. 357.

[22.]   Port located along the south-western or Malabar Coast. It remained under Portuguese rule from 1503 to 1663, after which Cochin was ceded to the VOC. See JDC, p. 358.

[23.]   See the glossary (*Mylapur*).

[24.]   Kingdom located at the northern shore of the Bay of Bengal and now largely divided between India and Bangladesh. Bengal was conquered by the Moghuls in 1576 who governed the province (via the Nawab of Bengal) with varying degrees of self-administration and control.

[25.]   A *colcha* is a fine cotton (and more specifically a cotton and silk) embroidered cloth produced in Bengal and used by the Portuguese as wall hangings or bedspreads. See JDC, p. 316.

[26.]   A red-coloured gum used as a varnish; red lac.

ships went to China and to Japan, and another two came yearly from the Maluku Islands, laden with cloves for Your Majesty, which was [sent] as duties that those lands used to pay to Your Majesty.

All these vessels that I have mentioned came yearly to Melaka to trade and they paid the respective duties to Your Majesty. The Portuguese sold their textiles and bought spices and other commodities, and they loaded their ships and sailed to Goa and Cochin. Over there they again paid their duties to Your Majesty; this apart from the two ships laden with cloves that arrived on the account of Your Majesty. These were in addition to three or four ships that came yearly to Goa from China, laden with raw and twisted silk, many bolts of velvet, damasks, satin, taffetas, many *colchas*, marquees, and silk hangings to decorate homes, large quantities of musk, seed pearls, small pearls, together with large quantities of gold, camphor, China root, benzoin, alum stone, *tintinago*,[27] Chinese porcelain, sugar, and other commodities. Each of these carracks from China paid 50,000 or 60,000 *pardaus*[28] in taxes to Your Majesty at the customs and excise house in Goa. They then took from Goa to the north: [to] Chaul, Cambay, Diu,[29] Daman,[30] Muscat,[31] [and] Hormuz. They again paid exit duties for these products, and they again paid duties to His Majesty in Diu, Muscat, Hormuz, and other lands. [These were] in addition to the ships that came yearly to Portugal from India, which used to bring many spices. They also paid the exit duties for this merchandise that they brought.

---

27. A copper-zinc-nickel alloy used across different metallurgical industries, including the casting of cannonballs, musket shots or (church) bells. See also SMS, p. 338.
28. Equivalent to about 1.355 and 1.625 metric tons of coin-grade silver.
29. Port located on an island off north-west India. The Portuguese seized the port from the Sultan of Gujarat in 1535 and remained a Portuguese possession until 1961.
30. Port located on the north-western coast of India. It was taken from the sultan of Gujarat in 1523 and remained a Portuguese possession until 1961. See JDC, p. 359.
31. Trading port in present-day northern Oman on the Arabian Peninsula. Muscat was controlled by the Portuguese between 1507 and 1650. See JDC, p. 369.

Your Majesty has lost all this trade; which is now in the hands of the [Dutch] rebels. They have grown rich with this commerce and by means of their robberies, and the Portuguese in India have become impoverished with this significant loss. This is why Your Majesty should help and remedy that the Estado [da Índia] in the manner that I have described, so as not to lose these lands and the many Christian communities that there are in them.

Glossary

ambergris   (Also: *ambar* and other spellings). A baleen or whale product, not to be confused with amber, which is a fossilised resin. The term is of Arabic origin. Ambergris appears to be a natural excretion of the indigestible parts of the whale's diet. When tumbled on the sea as flotsam and exposed to the sun, the melanin washes out and the ambergris appears whitish in colour. Ambergris was commonly collected along beaches where whales migrate. It contains an odoriferous resin that is uniquely sweet and pleasant. Ambergris was believed to possess certain medicinal properties and was commonly used in medicine, perfumery and as an ingredient for cooking and confectionary.[1]

bendahara   (Also: *bendara*). A high-ranking, hereditary position in a Malay polity that in more recent times has become synonymous to the "chief minister" and "minister of interior". He came first in precedence after the ruler (*shah*, *sultan*). According to the *Undang-undang Melaka* (Laws of Melaka), a legal code that retained authority in Malay polities throughout most of the early modern period, the *bendahara* was specifically

---

[1]   BOC, I.2, p. 692; BOC, II.3, p. 600; GVOC, p. 12; JDC, p. 301; SMS, p. 337; Borschberg, "O comércio de âmbar asiático no início da época moderna (séculos XV–XVIII)—The Asiatic Ambergris trade in the early modern period (15th to 18th century)", *Revista Oriente* 8 (2004): 3–25. "Der Asiatische Ambra-Handel während der frühen Neuzeit", *Mirabilia Asiatica II*, ed. Jorge Alves, Claude Guillot and Roderich Ptak (Wiesbaden and Lisbon: Harrassowitz-Fundação Oriente, 2004), pp. 167–201.

given "jurisdiction for instance[s] over those who are holding office, and those who rank as *tuan* [lord] or *sida* (court officers) and the children of high dignitaries." The *bendahara* importantly also served as the master of ceremonies (such as the *sirih nobat* ceremony, the serving of betel and playing of the royal orchestra in the presence of the *bendahara*). He legitimised activities at the court through ritual. The *bendahara* also received gifts from foreign traders coming to Melaka as well as from emissaries of foreign rulers. In Portuguese Melaka, the *bendahara* evolved into a representative of the non-Christian, non-Muslim communities of Melaka (such as notably the Hindus and Buddhists), while his counterpart, the *temenggong* (see separate entry), became the representative of the Muslims. In late-16th and early-17th-century Johor, the *bendahara* was, together with the *laksamana* (see separate entry), one of the most important "merchants" or "merchant-officials".[2]

bezoar   (Malay: *guliga*). Concrements ("stones") found in different parts of the intestinal tracts of mammals, especially in ruminants. When harvested from monkeys (so-called monkey stones), they are generally the gall stone found in the ape. Bezoar stones are not exactly the most sightly of objects to look upon, but their potential value as a life-saving medication and panacea in almost all medication in Europe of the early modern period rendered them more costly than diamonds. For this reason, jewellers—such as De Coutre who appears to have been very knowledgeable about bezoars—dealt in this most costly of Asian rare commodities. In traditional cultures of Arabia, Europe, India, and the Indianised cultures of Southeast Asia, bezoars are also believed to possess magical or mystical properties

---

[2.]   CMJ, pp. 461–2; GLA I, pp. 115–6; GVOC, p. 18; HJ, p. 84; JDC, pp. 305–6; PSM, pp. 155, 178–9, 203–13, 338; SMS, p. 334, Liaw Yock Fang, ed., *Undang-Undang Melaka. A Critical Edition* (The Hague: De Nederlandsche Boek-en Steendrukkerij / Verlagshuis S.L. Smits, 1976), pp. 62–3; Muhammad Yusof Hashim, *The Malay Sultanate of Malacca*, tr. D.J. Muzaffar Tate (Kuala Lumpur: Dewan Bahasa dan Pustaka, 1992), pp. 28–34.

to ward off spells and many forms of evil. In the early modern period, bezoars were often treated like precious stones. Just as is the case with diamonds and other known (cut or polished gems), they were sold by the carat, and the price per carat rose exponentially.[3]

camphor

(Arabic: *kafur*; Malay: *kapur*). A type of tree or its white resin found between the bark and the tree trunk. In the early modern period there were fundamentally two types of camphor traded: natural tropical camphor (sometimes also called "Barus camphor" or "edible camphor") and synthetically produced Japanese laurel camphor. The latter can only be applied externally (on the skin) to treat bites and certain skin disorders. It was cheap and plentifully produced in China. By contrast, tropical camphor from Borneo or Sumatra was not toxic when ingested and was widely used in Asian as well as European pharmacology during the early modern period. Tropical camphor was most commonly used as a remedy against intestinal parasites. While the Arabs and Indians (mainly Gujaratis) chiefly procured their tropical camphor at the ports of Barus or Pariaman located on the western coast of Sumatra, the Chinese purchased their supplies from Borneo. Jan Huyghen van Linschoten claimed that the camphor from Borneo was the best in all of Asia. Tropical camphor was priced at about one hundred times its synthetic counterpart.[4]

captain

(Portuguese: *capitão*). First and foremost a military rank. With reference to early Portuguese colonial expansion in general, it should be highlighted that the chief administrators of forts and colonies usually held the rank of an army captain (or sometimes captain-major). For this reason, some early modern sources refer to the "captain" of a given fort or settlement as its "governor". See also the separate entry for *captain-major*.[5]

[3.] BOC, I.1, p. 728; BOC, III, p. 587; EFS, II, p. 1395; GLA, I, pp. 107–9; GVOC, p. 20; HJ, pp. 90–1; JDC, pp. 307–8.
[4.] CMJ, p. 465; EFS, II, p. 1396; JDC, p. 311.
[5.] CMJ, p. 466.

captain-major	(Portuguese: *capitão-mór*). A commander of a fleet comprising several large vessels. The title is applied to captains who temporarily have other captains under their command or allegiance, such as during a military campaign. The title was often also assigned to the headmen of informal (non-official) Portuguese settlements. See also the separate entry for *captain*.[6]
carrack	A large and generally lightly-armed Portuguese trading ship of the 16th and early 17th centuries. The carrack's design characteristically features a forecastle and an elevated poop deck. The term was sometimes also employed as a synonym for galleon.[7]
coltois	Portuguese term employed by Afonso de Albuquerque for the title of "emperor" assumed or attributed to the monarchs of Melaka in the time of the sultanate. This word is most likely a corruption of the Malay term *ketua* (senior, elder, leader; here the lead or senior king) but it could be a derivative of the Malay expression *kedatuan* (kraton, palace, empire). The word *datu* appears to be an older equivalent of the Indian *raja*, and for this reason Dutch scholar Johannes Gijsbertus de Casparis translated the expression *kedatuan* as "the empire as a whole"—its ruler would have therefore been the ruler of the "empire as a whole". See also the separate entry for *Emperor of the Malays*.[8]
Emperor of the Malays	In Europe during the Middle Ages, the title "emperor" was conferred only to the Holy Roman Emperor who claimed to be the legal successor of the emperor of ancient Christian Rome (and later also from its eastern offshoot, Byzantium). By the 16th century the usage of this title had become

---

6. CMJ, p. 466; JDC, p. 312.
7. BOC, I.1, p. 739; DLM, pp. 368–9; HJ, pp. 165–6; JDC, p. 313.
8. J.G. de Casparis, ed., *Prasasti Indonesia: Selected Inscriptions from the 7th to the 9th Centuries AD* (Bandung: Masa Baru, 1956), the Old Malay Inscription of Tĕlaga Batu (South Sumatra), p. 18n10, 11; also "kedatuanku" (my empire), pp. 35, 43.

more flexible, and in the period of early expansion was also applied to monarchs outside Europe who ruled over vast regions and different peoples. The Dutch, for example, used the term *keizer* (emperor) as the title for the ruler of Brunei whom they commonly referred to as the "Emperor of Borneo". Jane Drakard makes a similar observation with regard to the ruler of the Minangkabau, whom the Dutch also referred to as "emperor". In line with this loose, less stringent employment of this European title are Spanish and Portuguese references to the "Emperor of the Malay Kings". The *Comentários de Afonso de Albuquerque* (Commentaries of Afonso de Albuquerque), compiled and published by his son Brás de Albuquerque in 1557, also mentioned this title, claiming that the rulers of the Melaka Sultanate "became in time so powerful, that they were called *coltois* (which appears to be a corruption or derivative of the Malay word *ketua*), a word used among them for "emperor". It must be immediately adjoined here that the term "Malay kings" was not employed by De Albuquerque in this specific context, the title was simply attributed to the rulers of precolonial Melaka. Similarly, De Coutre explained: "The king [of Johor is called Raja Ali [Jalla bin Abdul Jalil]. His grandfather was once the king of Melaka … He used the title … 'Emperor of the Malays'." This usage for Raja Ali Jalla is confirmed by a letter, dated 28 November 1587, written in Portuguese by Dom Paulo de Lima Pereira and addressed to King Philip II/I of Spain and Portugal. The title employed in this document translates into English as "Emperor of the Malay Kings". As De Coutre, however, continued to explain in one of his memorials, that title lapsed on the death of Raja Ali Jalla in 1597 and "had not been revived". Leonard Andaya has associated the title of "Malay Emperor" with the term *Maharaja di Raja* (great king of kings), "a title infused with the supernatural powers attributed to the legendary Adit Yawarman." The disuse of this title may very well be connected to the multipolarity of the Batu Sawar court and to the

Acehnese invasion of Aru, Johor, Pahang and other parts of the Malay Peninsula after the death of Raja Ali Jalla. See also the separate entry for *coltois*.[9]

Estado da Índia Literally translates to the "State of India". This term collectively refers to the patchwork of Portuguese colonial dependencies around the Indian Ocean rim and the Western Pacific that were administered from Goa. The *Estado da Índia* was made up of a string of forts and ports and sometimes larger territories that were subject to different degrees of authority, ranging from outright sovereign possessions to forts and ports under contract with neighbouring Asian or African rulers. The expression is often used interchangeably with "Portuguese India", *Asia Portuguesa*, as well as its colonial administration and bureaucracy.[10]

factor, factory Resident head of a so-called factory (sometimes called "lodge" or "house" in VOC sources). The term is of Italian or Portuguese origin and in earliest times referred to a commercial agent or the head of a collection and billing station. In the context of East Indian trade, however, the *feitoria* or "factory" was often a heavily fortified structure with a resident population rendering support services to the factory and its broader activities. These settlements were usually beyond, or specifically exempted from, the jurisdiction of the local Asian overlord by treaty. The factor was in charge of the entire operations within a given compound, and in the case of larger settlements also oversaw public works.[11]

laksamana (Also: *lassamane, lacamane* and other spellings). A Malay title or office holder corresponding approximately to

---

9.   CMJ, pp. 474–6; GPFT, pp. 365–6n66; JDC, pp. 94, 187n14, 364; SMS, pp. 226, 323n155; Borschberg, "Jacques de Coutre as a Source", p. 90n97; L.Y. Andaya, *Leaves of the Same Tree: Trade and Ethnicity in the Straits of Melaka* (Honolulu: Hawai'i University Press, 2008), p. 104; Jane Drakard, *A Kingdom of Words: Language and Power in Sumatra* (Oxford: Oxford University Press, 1999), pp. 24, 75, 121, 125, 134–5.
10. SMS, p. 335.
11. CMJ, p. 476; GVOC, p. 42; HJ, pp. 345–7; JDC, pp. 320–1.

the commander of the fleet or admiral. According to Muhammad Yusof Hashim, the office of the *laksamana* was the fourth highest official in precedence after the *bendahara*. The office of the *laksamana*, moreover, had been created during the period of the Melaka Sultanate, deriving his powers substantially from the *hulubalang besar* (captain-in-chief), a title generally associated in history with the Sri Bija di Raja and Singapore. During the period of the Melaka Sultanate (and certainly later in Johor), the *laksamana* was according to Muhammad Yusof "responsible for protocol and foreign embassies. However, his main duties were related to the military." The *Undang-undang Melaka* described the *laksamana* as the *raja laut* (king or lord of the sea). He served as fleet commander and that implied commander of the *orang laut* naval forces. During the Johor Sultanate the *laksamana,* as well as the Johorese armada, appear to have been based in Singapore. In Aceh the *laksamana* was reportedly also responsible for dealing with foreign merchants, similar to the *shahbandar* in other ports. The Portuguese chronicler João de Barros called this Malay official the "captain-major of the sea" (*capitão-mór do mar*). In late 16th and early 17th century Johor, the *laksamana* was together with the *bendahara* one of the most important "merchants" or "merchant-officials". Charles Otto Blagden described the title of *laksamana* as "roughly equivalent to Admiral, to which certain administrative and court duties on shore were attached." In one instance the travelogue of Dutch Admiral Cornelis Matelieff ascribed the functions of an admiral to the *temenggong* of Johor.[12]

musk   (Also: black musk). Used to designate many types of odoriferous substances, of both animal and plant origin. In the early modern period, however, the expression was employed almost exclusively to signify the natural excretion of the Asian musk deer inhabiting China, Siberia and the Himalayan range. In

---

[12.]   CMJ, p. 490; GLA, I, pp. 516–7, II, p. 502; GVOC, p. 67; JDC, p. 327; SMS, p. 335.

the early modern period, musk was used in perfumes, as a medicine, and sometimes also as an ingredient for baked goods and confectionery.[13]

orang laut   (Also: sea nomad; sea gypsy). The Portuguese and Spanish name commonly used is *selates* or *saletes*, the latter of which is rooted in the Malay word *selat* meaning "strait". Thus the *selates* are the people who live in or around the *selat* or strait. In English, the term "sea gypsy" was used in the past, but is now considered a pejorative. *Orang laut* translates from the Malay language as "people of the sea". In precolonial times the *orang laut* were loyal to the Melaka sultan, but later they paid allegiance to the sultan of Johor, at least until the end of the Melaka dynasty toward the end of the 17th century. They often served as the sultan's navy, patrolled the Straits and acted as paid pilots to passing European, Chinese and Arab vessels. The Portuguese chronicler João de Barros claimed that the *celates* "lived afloat rather than on land. Their sons were born and bred on the sea and had no fixed bases ashore."[14]

raja   A term of Sanskrit origin meaning "king". Historically the title was deployed in a very elastic manner, spanning from a great king in India (*maharaja*) to a petty prince in Southeast Asia. The title of *raja* was commonly used on the Indian subcontinent as well as in the Indianised regions of insular and peninsular Southeast Asia, and remained in use well after the advent of Islam in the region. As Hans Hägerdal has noted, "In the case of Southeast Asia, the foreign visitors may have

---

[13.]   EFS, II, p. 1405; GLA, I, p. 27; JDC, pp. 330, 340; SMS, p. 337; Borschberg, "The European Musk Trade with Asia in the Early Modern Period", *Revista Oriente* 5 (2003): 90–9; "Der asiatische Moschushandel vom frühen 15. bis zum 17. Jahrhundert", *Mirabilia Asiatica*, ed. Jorge Alves, Claude Guillot and Roderich Ptak (Wiesbaden and Lisbon: Harrassowitz-Fundação Oriente, 2003), pp. 65–84.

[14.]   BOC, II.3, p. 613; EFS, II, p. 1406; GVOC, p. 83; HJ, pp. 644–5; JDC, pp. 336–7; SMS, pp. 335–6; David E. Sopher, *The Sea Nomads, a Study Based on Literature of the Maritime Boat People of Southeast Asia* (Singapore: Lim Bian Han, 1965); Oliver W. Wolters, *Early Indonesian Commerce: A Study of the Origins of Srivijaya* (Ithaca: Cornell University Press, 1967), p. 222 (citing Barros).

followed the Malay use of the term *raja*, which has a much wider usage than to simply denote autonomous monarchs". In a very similar vein Richard Chauvel noted with reference to Ambon: "Outside Ambon town, with a few exceptions, Moslems and Christians live in separate *negeri* each with their own *raja* (village head) and administration, sharing a common *adat* (customary law)." Dutch and Portuguese sources of the 16th and 17th centuries commonly referred to the Malay rulers as "*rajas*", by the Persian-Moghul title "*shah*", or translate the title into their own language, as for example *raya*, *rayale* or *koninck*. The title "sultan", by contrast, appears to have established itself fairly late. As William Roff has highlighted, the "personal honorific of sultan, known in the Malay states since the coming of Islam, was not widely used in the nineteenth century, though it achieved general currency thereafter." See also the separate entry for *Emperor of the Malays*.[15]

Raja Bongsu	A Malay title meaning the "Young" or "Junior King"; *bongsu* being an endearing term in Malay referring to the youngest child. Raja Bongsu, who himself was to rule as sultan of Johor between 1613/5 and 1623 as Abdullah Ma'ayat Shah, was also variously known as Raja Seberang and Raja di Ilir. At the time of VOC Admiral Cornelis Matelieff's seaborne attack on Portuguese Melaka (1606) and later during his visit to the Batu Sawar court, political power in Johor appears to have been multipolar, and effectively divided between the four surviving sons of Raja Ali Jalla bin Abdul Jalil. This division of power is said to have been engineered by the Bendahara Paduka Raja,

---

[15.] CMJ, pp. 506–7; JDC, pp. 336–7; Richard Chauvel, "Ambon's Other Half: Some Preliminary Observations on Ambonese Society and History", *Review of Indonesian and Malaysian Affairs* 14, 1 (1980): 40–80, esp. p. 41; Hans Hägerdal, *Lords of the Land, Lords of the Sea: Conflict and Adaptation in Early Colonial Timor, 1600–1800* (Leiden: KITLV Press, 2012), p. 52; W.R. Roff, *The Origins of Malay Nationalism* (Kuala Lumpur and Singapore: University of Malaya Press, 1967), p. 2.

Tun Sri Lanang. Although 'Ala'uddin formally held the title of *shah* (king), many of the affairs of state—including especially foreign relations (and that would include waging war)—were apparently the purview of Raja Bongsu. As is further evident from the writings of Matelieff, Raja Bongsu had an *istana* (palace, residence) and vassals at Kota Seberang, a settlement located across the river and slightly downstream from Batu Sawar. W.G. Shellabear has identified the location as Pengkalan Lama. In addition to Kota Seberang, Raja Bongsu is also said to have had a personal fiefdom in Sambas on the great island of Borneo. Various issues concerning the genealogy of Raja Bongsu have been historicised and problematised, among others, by Cheah Boon Kheng and Paulo Pinto.[16]

Raja Siak   There is mixed but generally negative information about this individual whom Pieter Gerritsz Rouffaer has positively identified as Raja Hasan of Siak. Matelieff's *Historische Verhael* claims that the Raja Siak was one of the four surviving sons of the Raja Ali Jalla bin Abdul Jalil. Elisa Netscher, who probably used Commelin or another printed edition of Matelieff's voyage as his source for compiling materials in *De Nederlanders in Djohor en Siak* (The Dutch in Johor and Siak) read the passage from Matelieff to mean Raja Siak was an illegitimate brother of Ala'uddin. By contrast, the travelogue of Admiral Matelieff's voyage to Asia asserts that 'Ala'uddin, Raja Bongsu and Raja Laut were born of different "wives" of Raja Ali Jalla, and the same holds true for Raja Siak. Such a reference could also be taken

---

[16.] JDC, p. 337; PSM, pp. 238–55; P.G. Leupe, "The Siege and Capture of Malacca from the Portuguese in 1640–1641. Extracts from the Archives of the Dutch East India Company", tr. Mac Hacobian, *JMBRAS* 14, 1 (1936): 149. See also Cheah Boon Kheng and Peter Borschberg, "Raja Bongsu and *Sejarah Melayu* (The Malay Annals): An 'ill-starred prince' of Johor with a tragic fate (b. 1571– d. 1623)", forthcoming, *JMBRAS* 2015; and W.G. Shellabear, *Sejarah Melayu* [The Malay Annals], 9th ed. (Singapore: Malaya Publishing House, 1961), p. 264: "… Raja 'Abdullah beristana diseberang Pengkalan Raya, maka disebut orang Raja Seberang" (Raja 'Abdullah whose palace was across the river in Pengkalan Raya, is called by others Raja Seberang).

to mean a concubine rather than a legitimate wife. The Standish-Croft Journal relating to Thomas Best's voyage to the East Indies regarded the Raja Siak not as a natural (half-) sibling, but rather as a brother-in-law. This is not likely, however, as Raja Siak had wed a daughter of Raja Hijau of Patani in late 1602 or early 1603. Best's statement also does not conform to a letter penned by Raja Bongsu and King 'Ala'uddin in 1609 addressed to Prince Maurice, the Stadholder of Holland and Zeeland.[17]

seligi   (Sometimes also *saligi*). During the late 16th and early 17th centuries the traveller Pedro Teixeira defined the *saliga* or *seligi* as follows: "But the commonest [weapons] are salikhes, which are charred stakes, so hard as to pierce like iron; and easily broken, whereupon they have the wound full of a thousand splinters that make it most incurable." His contemporary Manoel Godinho de Erédia mentions *soligues* in both his *Report on the Golden Chersonese* (c. 1597–1600) as well as in his *Description of Malacca* (c. 1613) and described them as "darts ... with which the [orang laut] transfixed the fish swimming at the bottom of the sea." In addition to using these to stun fish, *seligis* were also deployed in warfare, as is confirmed by Barreto de Resende around 1638.[18]

shahbandar   (Also: *chiabandaer*, *shahbunder*, *xabandar* and other spellings). A term of Persian origin meaning "king of the port", loosely also "port master" or "harbour master"; common to the Malay Archipelago, the Indian subcontinent and around the western Indian Ocean. In Malay polities, the term denotes a high-ranking official

---

[17] CMJ, pp. 509–10; W. Foster, ed., *The Voyage of Thomas Best to the East Indies 1612–1614* (London: Hakluyt Society, 1934), p. 169. On the definitive linkage of Raja Siak with Hasan, see Pieter Gerritsz. Rouffaer, "Was Malaka Emporium vóór 1400 A.D. genaamd Malajoer? En waar lag Woerawari, Ma-Hasin, Langka, Batoesawar?", *Bijdragen en Mededelingen van het Koninklijk Instituut voor Taal-, Land- und Volkenkunde* 77 (1921): 445n1.

[18] GLA, II, p. 277; Erédia, *Description of Malaca, Meridional India and Cathay*, ed. and tr. J.V. Mills (Kuala Lumpur: MBRAS, 1997), pp. 16, 90, 232.

of state who issued maritime passes (*licentmeester*, license master) and as a rule also acted as an intermediary between the ruler and foreign merchants. (The notable exception is in Aceh; see the separate entry for *laksamana*). The *shahbandar* held considerable powers to arbitrate disputes involving foreign merchants. According to the *Undang-undang Melaka* (Laws of Melaka), the *shahbandar* was "given jurisdiction over all matters concerning foreign merchants, orphans and all who have suffered injustice, and furthermore, the regulations pertaining to junks, cargo-boats and other vessels." The title was equally applied to the port masters of towns situated inland along major rivers, such as for example in Batu Sawar and Johor Lama. In Portuguese Melaka, the *shahbandar* was importantly also responsible for reselling rice to the city's residents. The *shahbandar* was often a foreigner who enjoyed the trust and confidence of a local ruler, and for this reason he is reported to have supervised imports and the warehousing of imported goods as well as investments of the ruler or members of the royal family. In the Melaka Sultanate there were a total of four *shahbandars* who held jurisdiction over the principal ethnic communities that were active in the city's commerce, but this number was incidentally not stipulated by the *Undang-undang Melaka* (Laws of Melaka).[19]

temenggong   (Also: *tamungo* and other spellings). A high-ranking Malay official in charge of security, prisons and customs. According to the *Undang-undang Melaka* (Laws of Melaka), the *temenggong* (the title has been translated into English as "police chief") was given "jurisdiction over crimes committed in the country [*di dalam negeri*] and (matters) such as the investigation (of crime) and the apprehension of criminals in the land [*di dalam negeri*]." This office was later also adopted and adapted

---

[19.]   BOC, III, p. 593; CMJ, pp. 509–10; EFS, II, p. 1409; GLA, II, pp. 419–20; GVOC, pp. 69, 106; HJ, p. 816; JDC, pp. 342–3; Leupe, "The Siege and Capture of Malacca", p. 126; Tomé Pires, *The Suma Oriental of Tome Pires: An Account of the East from the Red Sea to Japan. Written in Malacca and India in 1512–1515*, ed. Armando Cortesão, 2 vols. (London: Hakluyt Society, 1944), II, p. 265.

by the Portuguese during the colonial period before 1641. Under the Portuguese, however, the office of the *temenggong* evolved into a representative of the Muslim community while his counterpart, the *bendahara*, acted as the representative of the non-Christian, non-Muslim communities such as the Hindus and the Buddhists. According to the *Relação das Plantas & Descripções de todas as Fortalezas, Cidades & Povoações que os Portuguezes tem no Estado da India Oriental* (Commentary on the Maps and Descriptions of all of the Fortresses, Cities and Townships which the Portuguese have in the oriental *Estado da Índia*) the *temenggong* of Portuguese Melaka was appointed by the viceroy in Goa and derived a ten per cent revenue from the king of Johor's Muslim subjects in and around Melaka.[20]

viagem   (Plural: *viagens*; lit. "voyage"). The exclusive concession by the Portuguese crown to organise voyages between two specific ports for a limited and specified period, generally between one and three years. The *viagens* were conceded for voyages starting and terminating in Goa, Melaka and later also Macao for destinations across maritime Southeast Asia (notably the Malukus), China, Japan and Africa. The *viagens* were sometimes sold and at other times granted by royal favour as a reward for past services to the crown.[21]

VOC   *Vereenigde Oostindische Compagnie* (VOC) or the United Netherlands Chartered East India Company or Dutch East India Company. Formed in 1602 by merging six regional trading companies, the company was given a wide range of powers through its charter from the Dutch States General. These included the right to enter into treaties and alliances, wage war, levy troops, build forts, appoint governors, and pronounce justice. After 1619 its administrative centre in Asia was centred in Batavia (formerly known as Jayakerta or Jacatra) on the northern coast of Java.[22]

---

[20]   CMJ, pp. 518–9; GLA, II, 350; PSM, pp. 178–9, 203–13, 340; *Relação das Plantas*, p. 44.

[21]   JDC, p. 347; PSM, p. 340.

[22]   JDC, p. 348.

List of Place Names

Aru   Widely considered by early 16th-century Portuguese sources to be a nation of sea-raiding plunderers. There can be little doubt that it represented politically and economically a competitor to both Melaka and later to Johor. Denys Lombard has reported that Aru had been taken by Aceh in 1564, but the exact status of Aru after this is vague. It would appear that the ruler of Aru refused submission to Aceh or briefly freed himself of it. By the early 17th century it was described as an ally of Johor. Aru was again attacked in 1613 (the same year as Aceh's offensive against Batu Sawar) and it would appear that hereafter a vanquished Aru finally accepted submission to Aceh and was subsequently known as Deli. António Bocarro mentioned the "Isles of Aru" (*ileus Daru*), which appears to refer to the islands located off the eastern coast of Sumatra around Bengkalis.[1] See also the map on p. 74.

Batu Sawar   The administrative centre and capital of Johor in the final years of the 16th and early 17th century. Located in the upper reaches of the Johor River it is described by De Coutre as a key trading centre and a home to many

---

[1]   CMJ, p. 529; JDC, pp. 351–2; D. Lombard, *Le Sultanat d'Atjéh au temps d'Iskandar Muda 1607–1636* (Paris: École français d'Extrême-Orient, 1967), pp. 37, 83, 92; Anthony C. Milner, E. Edwards McKinnon and Tengku Luckman Sinar, "Aru and Kota Cina", *Indonesia* 26 (1978): 1–42.

merchants. Batu Sawar was important in the context of the pepper trade, and the bezoars and diamonds trade. It would appear that De Coutre traded both bezoars and diamonds in Batu Sawar.[2]

Beruas, also Baroas

Probably a corruption of the Malay name "Beruas" or "Bruas" which means "wild mango". A Kampung Beruas is still located today close to the sea at the Pahang River estuary and forms a suburb of the royal capital Pekan. De Coutre claims that he landed here on a trip from Melaka in 1594, and that its inhabitants were subjects of the king of Pahang.[3]

Borneo

In the early modern period, this name refers to either the island of Borneo; a polity (a precursor of present-day Brunei), or a port (in present-day Brunei Bay). De Coutre visited the port of Borneo and describes the settlement and the palace of the ruler who in contemporaneous 17th-century sources is sometimes titled the "Emperor of Borneo". This was an important trading centre for jungle produce and especially for tropical camphor, diamonds and bezoars.[4]

Jayakerta

(Also *Jayakarta*, *Jacatra*, renamed *Batavia* in 1619; present-day Jakarta). City on the island of Java. Before Jayakerta became the base for the VOC's Asian operations in 1619, it was known as Sunda Kelapa and after 1527 as Jayakerta (Sanskrit for "Complete Victory"). The city rose to prominence in the late 16th and early 17th century under Pangeran Wijayakrama (alias Jayawikarta), who was loyal to Banten and had established his residence near the Ciliwung River estuary. The Prince granted permission to the Dutch in 1610 to establish a wooden warehouse along the right (eastern) bank of the Ciliwung River. Five years later the East India Company of London (EIC) was granted the same privilege for the left (western) river bank. The

---

[2.] CMJ, p. 532; JDC, p. 353; SMS, p. 342.
[3.] JDC, p. 353.
[4.] CMJ, p. 535; JDC, p. 354.

prince's political manoeuvring with the English and the Dutch eventually led to his downfall. The city was taken by the VOC and renamed Batavia in 1619.[5]

Johor Lama

(Also: *Jor* or *Yor Viejo*). Served as the royal residence and capital of Johor until it was sacked during a military campaign led by Dom Paulo de Lima Pereira in 1587. Johor Lama or Old Johor is located on the left bank in the lower reaches of the Johor River. Documents of the 17th century report that the city was rebuilt, destroyed again around 1604, and rebuilt a second time. When the Johor court moved to the upstream town of Batu Sawar, Johor Lama continued to be used as a port where larger, ocean-going vessels would anchor and transfer their cargo to smaller vessels (for example *perahus* or *sampans*). From here the goods were brought to the upstream towns such as the royal administrative centre of Batu Sawar and the nearby settlement of Kota Seberang on the opposite bank of the Johor River.[6]

Karimun

There are technically two Karimuns: Karimun Besar (Great Carimon) and the far smaller and uninhabited Karimun Kecil (Carimon Minor). The Karimuns are located between the great island of Sumatra and the Malay Peninsula. They are strategically located, as several major shipping routes converge around the islands, including significantly the Singapore, Melaka, Durian and Kundur Straits (the latter being known as the Strait of Sabam from Portuguese source materials).[7]

Lawai

(Also: *Lave, Lava, Lavio, Lawei*). A river and port along the southern coast of Borneo in the present-day Indonesian province of West Kalimantan. Its exact location is not known, but may have been at or around the Kapuas River estuary. Another possibility is the Bay of Lavio (sometimes also Laio) between Sukadana and present-day Pontianak on the island of Borneo; yet another interpretation places it in Sukadana. Lawai was

---

5. CMJ, pp. 447–8; JDC, p. 364.
6. CMJ, p. 549; JDC, p. 365; SMS, p. 343.
7. CMJ, pp. 550–1; JDC, p. 376; SMS, p. 343.

together with Banjarmasin one of the most important ports on the island of Borneo. De Coutre mentioned a political connection with Johor.[8]

Makassar

(Also: *Macaçar, Macaçal; Macasar* and other spellings). A port (between 1971 to 1999 known as Ujung Pandang) and polity in the south of the great island of Sulawesi (Celebes). Makassar was important in the context of the seaborne trade and in the bulk trade in spices (cloves and nutmeg from the Malukus) and rice. In 1605 the ruler of Makassar converted to Islam and began a series of campaigns to control the region, conquering its main rival, Bone, in a campaign from 1608 to 1611. This was followed by campaigns against Sumbawa, Buru, Seram, Banten and eastern Borneo. In the early 17th century, Makassar became a base for many European traders and trading companies, including the English, Danes, and Portuguese, who sought to break the stranglehold of the Dutch in the spice trade. Makassar was defeated in a war against the Dutch in 1667.[9]

Maluku

(Also: *Maluco*; Moluccas, Spice Islands). Sub-group of the Indonesian Archipelago located between the two great islands of Sulawesi (Celebes) and Papua (New Guinea), comprising among others the clove and nutmeg producing islands of Ambon, Aru, Banda, Buru, Halmahera, Seram, Ternate, Tidore and others. The region is ethnically and culturally diverse, featuring among others Malay and Papuan influences. The islands were contested by the Portuguese and the Spanish, who sought to claim and extend their influence over the islands. In the early 17th century the contest for the Malukus involved the Dutch, who eventually came to dominate the entire archipelago and monopolised the spice trade in nutmeg, mace (a by-product of nutmeg) and cloves.[10]

[8.] DC, p 366.
[9.] CMJ, pp. 554–5; JDC, p. 367.
[10.] CMJ, p. 557; JDC, p. 368; SMS, p. 343.

Melaka	(Also: *Mallaqua*, Malacca and other spellings). Name variously given to the river, the town or city of Melaka, a polity centred around the city (Melaka Sultanate), as well as in European cartography to the whole Malay Peninsula. The name has also been applied to the nearby maritime strait (the Malacca or Melaka Strait). Believed by the Portuguese to be one of the most— some might contend the most—important centre(s) of trade in the East Indies by the early 15th century, the Portuguese attacked and seized the city and some surrounding lands in 1511. Although Portuguese rule over Melaka was contested by Asian and other European parties such as Aceh, the Dutch, and also Johor, the Portuguese held on to the city until January 1641, when it succumbed to famine, pestilence and a protracted military campaign.[11]
Mylapur	(Also: *Melapor, Mellapor, Meliapore*). City situated on the Coromandel Coast in the present-day Indian State of Tamil Nadu close to Chennai (Madras); its full name in Portuguese is São Tomé de Meliapore. In 1522, the Portuguese discovered here what they believed was the grave of Saint Thomas the Apostle; his relics were transferred from here to Goa. As De Coutre rightly pointed out, this city is commonly known by two different names: São Tomé or Mylapur.[12]
New Strait of Singapore	(Portuguese: *Estreito Novo*). A maritime route, which according to the testimony of João de Barros opened up after the 1580s when Johor had blockaded the Old Strait (see the separate entry below) with logs, debris and sunken vessels. This route, also known from João de Barros in Portuguese as the *Estreito de Santa Barbara* (Strait of Santa Barbara) brought vessels during the age of sail along the south-western coast of present-day Sentosa and then either through the Buran Channel or

---

[11] CMJ, pp. 559–60; JDC, p. 367; SMS, pp. 157–88; Borschberg, "Ethnicity, Language and Culture in Melaka during the Transition from Portuguese to Dutch Rule", *JMBRAS* 83, 2 (2010): 93–117.

[12] JDC, pp. 369, 379.

around the southern islands and on to the region of the Johor River estuary.[13]

Old Strait of Singapore

(Portuguese: *Estreito Velho*; Old Strait of Singapore). This refers to the stretch of water between present-day Sentosa and Harbourfront. The western entrance to the Old Strait of Singapore begins at the site of present-day Fort Siloso (on the Sentosa side) and the *Varela* (also Longyamen, Sail Rock, Batu Belayer, Batu Blair, Lot's Wife) in today's Labrador Park. It continued through the narrow maritime passage between Sentosa and the old Keppel Harbour area and ended after Pulau Brani.[14]

Pahang

Polity, port and river located in south-eastern Peninsular Malaysia. In the late 16th and early 17th centuries, Pahang was considered a "vassal" or client state of Johor. It was famous chiefly for its pepper, gold dust (panned from the river beds) and bezoar stones. It was also important on account of the riverine trading network that linked to two coastal towns of Pahang (east) and Muar (west). According to early 17th-century sources, Pahang was a political dependency of Johor and assumed an important position in the pepper trade.[15]

Patani

Port and polity located on the Isthmus of Kra at the Gulf of Siam in present-day Thailand. Descriptions of the polity dating from the late 16th and early 17th centuries claimed that most of the eastern coast of the Malay Peninsula fell under the control of Patani, being chiefly the present-day Malaysian states of Kelantan and Terengganu. Many Chinese came to trade in Patani and brought a range of trading goods such as silks, copperware and porcelain. The town manufactured among other things neat clothing which were exported to and very much prized in Banda and the Maluku islands.[16]

---

13. CJM, p. 578; JDC, pp. 360–1; SMS, pp. 31–2.
14. CMJ, p. 578; JDC, p. 361; SMS, pp. 26–35.
15. CMJ, p. 566; JDC, pp. 372–3; SMS, p. 344.
16. JDC, p. 373.

Pulau Pisang   An islet and navigational landmark located off the south-western coast of the Malay Peninsula in the present-day Malaysian state of Johor. In 16th-century Portuguese cartography it is often named *Pula Pição* or *Pula Piçam* but actual spellings can vary considerably from source to source. This is not to be confused with an islet by almost the same name (in early modern European navigational literature) which is found off the coast of Pahang.[17] See also the maps on pp. 74, 83.

Sabandaria   (Also: *Xabandaria* and other spellings). This is the name given by Jacques de Coutre to the principal settlement on what he calls the *Isla de la Sabandaria Vieja* (present-day Singapore Island). According to his information, the settlement was located near the eastern entrance of the *Estrecho Viejo* (Old Strait of Singapore). He claimed that its inhabitants paid allegiance to the king of Johor. He also underscored that *Sabandaría*'s harbour was one of the best in all of the East Indies. The exact location of the settlement is unclear but it would have most likely been either at the site of Raffles' Landing Place (Singapore River) or possibly around the Kallang River estuary.[18]

South   Term generally employed by the Portuguese and the Spanish to refer to what today would be Southeast Asia, especially the insular portions of Indonesia and the Philippines. From the vantage point of the Portuguese administration in Goa, this region was located in the "South". Contemporary historians have variously translated this term into English either as "the South" (corresponding literally to the Portuguese *Sur* or the Spanish *Sul*), "the East Indies", or occasionally also as Southeast Asia.[19]

Strait of Kundur   (Also: *Estreito de Sabam*). An important maritime

---

17.   CMJ, p. 573; JDC, pp. 375–6.
18.   JDC, p. 378.
19.   CMJ, p. 579; JDC, p. 381.

artery in the early modern period that connected the southern reaches of the Melaka Strait with maritime routes to Palembang, Banten, key ports along the northern coast of Java, and additional destinations in the eastern regions of the Indonesian Archipelago, including Makassar, the Banda Islands, the Malukus and Timor. The Strait of Kundur extends from south to north between the eastern shores of Sumatra and the western shore of Kundur and Karimun Besar (Great Carimon).[20] See also the separate entry for *Karimun*.

Straits of Singapore   Portuguese: *Estreito* or *Estreitos de Sincapura*; also: *Syncapura*, *Sinquapura* and other spellings; present-day Straits of Singapore). A series of maritime passages that connect the Melaka Strait with the South China Sea along or near the shores of Singapore Island. In the early modern period there are three main passages, the best known being the Old Strait of Singapore.[21]

Tioman   (Present-day Tioman). An island located off the south-eastern coast of the Malay Peninsula. For centuries Tioman was a navigational landmark for ships sailing to or from the Vietnam Coast, China and Japan. Tioman reportedly had a thriving provisioning industry and ships took on food and fresh water before setting across the Gulf of Siam (or vice versa) to Pulau Condor (Vietnamese: Côn Sơn), the largest of a small group of islands located off the south-eastern coast of Vietnam.[22] Today, Tioman belongs to the Malaysian state of Pahang.

---

20. JDC, pp. 360, 378; SMS, p. 345.
21. CMJ, p. 578; JDC, p. 360–1.
22. CMJ, p. 584; JDC, pp. 376–7; SMS, p. 345.

Bibliography

Albuquerque, B. de, *The Commentaries of the Great A. Dalboquerque, Second Viceroy of India*, tr. Walter de Gray Birch, 4 vols. (London: Hakluyt Society, 1875–95).

Andaya, L.Y., *Leaves of the Same Tree: Trade and Ethnicity in the Straits of Melaka* (Honolulu: Hawai'i University Press, 2008).

Baker, C., "Review of 'The Memoirs and Memorials of Jacques de Coutre'", *Journal of the Siam Society* 102, 1 (2014): 294–6.

Baker, C., Dhiravat na Pombejra, A. van der Kraan and D.K. Wyatt, *Van Vliet's Siam* (Chiang Mai: Silkworm Books, 2005).

Barros, J. de and D. do Couto, *Da Ásia. Dos feitos que os Portuguezes fizeram no conquista, e descubrimento das terras e mares do Oriente*, 24 vols. (Lisbon: Na Regia Officina Typographia, 1777–78).

Borschberg, P., *The Singapore and Melaka Straits: Violence, Security and Diplomacy in the 17th Century* (Singapore and Leiden: NUS Press and KITLV Press, 2010).

——————, *Hugo Grotius, the Portuguese and Free Trade in the East Indies* (Singapore and Leiden: NUS Press and KITLV Press, 2011).

——————, ed., *The Memoirs and Memorials of Jacques de Coutre: Security, Trade and Society in 16th- and 17th-century Southeast Asia* (Singapore: NUS Press, 2014).

——————, ed., *Journal, Memorials and Letters of Cornelis Matelieff de Jonge: Security, Diplomacy and Commerce in 17th-century Southeast Asia* (Singapore: NUS Press, 2015).

————, "The Seizure of the *Sta. Catarina* Revisited: The Portuguese Empire in Asia, VOC Politics and the Origins of the Dutch-Johor Alliance (c. 1602–1616)", *JSEAS* 33, 1 (2002): 31–62.

————, "Der asiatische Moschushandel vom frühen 15. bis zum 17. Jahrhundert", in *Mirabilia Asiatica*, ed. J. Alves, C. Guillot and R. Ptak (Wiesbaden and Lisbon: Harrassowitz-Fundação Oriente, 2003), pp. 65–84.

————, "The European Musk Trade with Asia in the Early Modern Period", *Revista Oriente* 5 (2003): 90–9.

————, "Portuguese, Spanish and Dutch plans to construct a Fort in the Straits of Singapore ca 1584–1625", *Archipel* 65 (2003): 55–88.

————, "Der Asiatische Ambra-Handel während der frühen Neuzeit", in *Mirabilia Asiatica II*, ed. J. Alves, C. Guillot and R. Ptak (Wiesbaden and Lisbon: Harrassowitz-Fundação Oriente, 2004), pp. 167–201.

————, "The Asiatic Ambergris trade in the early modern period (15 to 18 century)", *Revista Oriente* 8 (2004): 3–25.

————, "A Portuguese-Dutch Naval Battle in the Johor River Estuary and the Liberation of Johor Lama in 1603", in *Early Singapore, 1300s– 1819: Evidence in Maps, Text and Artefacts,* ed. J.N. Miksic and C-A.M.G. Low (Singapore: History Museum, 2004), pp. 106–17.

————, "The Seizure of the *Santa Catarina* off Singapore: Dutch Freebooting, the Portuguese Empire and Intra-Asian Trade at the Dawn of the Seventeenth Century", *Revista de Cultura*, International Edition 11 (2004): 11–25.

————, "The Trade, Forgery and Medicinal Use of Porcupine Bezoars in the Early Modern Period (c. 1500–1750)", *Revista Oriente* 14 (2006): 60–78.

————, "The Euro-Asian Trade and Medicinal Usage of Radix Chinae", in *European Travellers and the Asian Natural World, Part 1*, ed. R.M. Loureiro, *Revista de Cultura*, International Edition 20 (2006): 102–15.

————, "Jacques de Coutre as a Source for the Early 17th Century History of Singapore, the Johor River, and the Straits", *JMBRAS* 81, 2 (2008): 71–97.

—————, "The Euro-Asian Trade in Bezoar Stones (approx. 1500–1700)", in *Artistic and Cultural Exchanges between Europe and Asia, 1400–1900: Rethinking Markets, Workshops and Collections,* ed. T. DaCosta Kaufmann and M. North (Aldershot: Ashgate, 2010), pp. 29–43.

—————, "Ethnicity, Language and Culture in Melaka during the Transition from Portuguese to Dutch Rule", *JMBRAS* 83, 2 (2010): 93–117.

—————, "From Self-Defence to an Instrument of War: Dutch Privateering Around the Malay Peninsula in the Early Seventeenth Century", *Journal of Early Modern History* 17 (2013): 35–52.

Briggs, L.P., "Spanish Intervention in Cambodia, 1593–1603", *T'oung Pao*, second series 39, 1/3 (1950): 132–60.

Brussels, Royal Library of Belgium, Ms. 39015A (*Manoel Godinho de Erédia, Description of Melaka*).

Campos, J. de, "Early Portuguese Accounts of Thailand", *Journal of the Siam Society* 32, 1 (1940): 1–28.

Casparis, J.G. de, *Prasasti Indonesia: Selected Inscriptions from the 7th and the 9th Centuries AD* (Bandung: Masa Baru, 1956).

Chauvel, R., "Ambon's Other Half: Some Preliminary Observations on Ambonese Society and History", *Review of Indonesian and Malaysian Affairs* 14, 1 (1980): 40–80.

Cheah B.K. and P. Borschberg, "Raja Bongsu and *Sejarah Melayu* (The Malay Annals): An 'ill-starred prince' of Johor with a tragic fate (b. 1571–d. 1623)", forthcoming, *JMBRAS* 2015.

Corte ende sekere Beschryvinghe vant veroveren der rijcke ende gheweldighe krake, comende uytet gheweste van China, door den Admirael Jacobus Heemskercke … (Ghedruckt na de copy van Middelborch by Richard Schilders, 1604).

Cortesão, A. and A.T. da Mota, *Portugaliae Monumenta Cartographica*, 9 vols. (Lisbon: Imprensa Nacional-Casa da Moeda, 1987).

Coutre, J. de, *Aziatische Omzwervingen. Het levensverhaal van Jaques de Coutre, een Brugs diamantenhandelaar, 1591–1626,* ed. and tr. J. Verbeckmoes and E. Stols (Berchem: EPO, 1988).

—————, *Como Remediar o Estado da Índia? Being the Appendices of the Vida de Jaques de Coutre (Madrid: Biblioteca Nacional, Ms. 2780)*, ed. B.N. Teesma (Leiden: Centre for the History of European Expansion, 1989).

—————, *Andanzas asiáticas*, ed. E. Stols, B.N. Teensma and J. Werbeckmoes (Madrid: História 16, 1991).

Dalgado, S.R., *Glosário Luso-Asiático*, 2 vols. (Coimbra: Imprensa da Universidade, 1919–21).

Dam, P. van, *Beschryvinge van de Oostindische Compagnie*, ed. F.W. Stapel, 8 vols. (The Hague: Martinus Nijhoff, 1931–43).

Dhiravat na Pombejra, *Siamese Court Life in the Seventeenth Century as Depicted in European Sources* (Bangkok: Chulalongkorn University, 2001).

Drakard, J., *A Kingdom of Words: Language and Power in Sumatra* (Oxford: Oxford University Press, 1999).

Erédia, M. Godinho de, *Malaca L'Inde Méridionale e le Cathay: Manuscrit original autographe de Godinho de Eredia appartenant à la Bibliothèque Royale de Bruxelles*, tr. M. Léon Janssen (Bruxelles: Librairie Européenne C. Muquardt, 1882).

—————, *Description of Malaca, Meridional India and Cathay*, ed. and tr. J.V. Mills (Kuala Lumpur: MBRAS, 1997).

Farrington, A., and Dhiravat na Pombejra, ed., *The English Factory in Siam, 1612–1685*, 2 vols. (London: The British Library, 2007).

Flores, M. da Conceição, *Os portugueses e o Sião no século XVI* (Lisbon: Impr. Nacional-Casa da Moeda, 1995).

Foster, W., ed., *The Voyage of Thomas Best to the East Indies 1612–1614* (London: Hakluyt Society, 1934).

Gibson-Hill, C.A., "Singapore Old Strait and New Harbour, 1300–1870", in *Memoirs of the Raffles Museum*, no. 3 (Singapore: Government Printing Office, 1956),

Hägerdal, Hans, *Lords of the Land, Lords of the Sea: Conflict and Adaptation in Early Colonial Timor, 1600–1800* (Leiden: KITLV Press, 2012).

Hulsius, L., ed., *Neundter Theil Orientalischer Indien, Darinnen begrieffen Ein kurtze Beschreibung einer Reyse, so von den Holländern unn Seeländern, in die Orientalischen Indien, mit neun grossen und vier kleinen Schiffen unter der Admiralschafft Peter Wilhelm Verhuffen in Jahren 1607, 1608 und 1609 verrichtet worden, neben Vermeldung, was ihnen fürnemlich auff solcher Reyse begegnet unnd zu Handen gangen. Auß kurtzer Verzeichnus Johann Verkens zusammengebracht und in Truck verfertigt durch M. Gotthard Arthus von Danzig* (Frankfurt: durch Matth. Beckern in Verlegung Iohannis Theodori de Bry, 1612).

Irwin, J., "Indian Textile Trade in the Seventeenth Century, II. Coromandel Coast", *Journal of Indian Textile History* 2 (1956): 24–42.

Irwin, J.I. and P.R. Schwartz, *Studies in Indo-European Textile History* (Ahmedabad: Calico Museum of Textile, 1966).

Jonge, J.K.J. de, *Opkomst van het Nederlandsch gezag in Oost-Indië: Verzameling van onuitgegeven stukken uit het oud-coloniaal archief*, 16 vols. (The Hague: Martinus Nijhoff, 1866–1925).

Leupe, P.G., "The Siege and Capture of Malacca from the Portuguese in 1640–1641. Extracts from the Archives of the Dutch East India Company", tr. Mac Hacobian, *JMBRAS* 14, 1 (1936): 1–178.

Liaw, Y.F., ed., *Undang-Undang Melaka. A Critical Edition*, Proefschrift Leiden (The Hague: De Nederlandsche Boek- en Steendrukkerij/ Verlagshuis S.L. Smits, 1976).

Linschoten, J.H. van, *Itinerario, Voyage ofte Schipvaert van Jan Huygen van Linschoten naer Oost ofte Portugaels Indien, 1579–1592*, and *Reys-geschrift vande navigatiën der Portugaloysers*, ed. H. Kern and J.C.M. Warnsinck, 2nd ed., 8 vols. (The Hague: Martinus Nijhoff, 1939).

Lobato, M., *Política e Comércio dos Portugueses na Insulíndia: Malaca e as Molucas de 1575 a 1605* (Macau: Instituto Português do Oriente, 1999).

———, "O cravo, as Molucas e os portugueses", in *A epopeia das especiarias*, ed. I. Guerreiro (Lisbon: IICT-Edições Inapa, 1999), pp. 104–30.

Lombard, D., *Le Sultanat d'Atjéh au temps d'Iskandar Muda 1607–1636* (Paris: École français d'Extrême-Orient, 1967).

London, British Library, WD 2973 (*Jackson, Batto Berlayer*).

————, Ms Add. 15737 fol. 10.

Loureiro, R.M., "European Encounters and Clashes in the South China Sea", II, *Revista de Cultura*, International Edition 12 (2004): 1–154.

MacGregor, I.A., "Notes on the Portuguese in Malaya", *JMBRAS* 28, 2 (1955): 5–47.

————, "Johore Lama in the Sixteenth Century", *JMBRAS* 28, 2 (1955): 48–125.

Madrid, National Library of Spain, Ms. 2780 (*Jacques de Coutre, Vida and the Memorials*).

Miksic, J.N., *Singapore and the Silk Road of the Sea, 1300–1800* (Singapore: NUS Press, 2013).

————, *Archeological Research on the "Forbidden Hill" of Singapore: Excavations at Fort Canning, 1984* (Singapore: National Museum, 1985).

Milner, A.C., E.E. McKinnon and Tengku Luckman Sinar, "Aru and Kota Cina", *Indonesia* 26 (1978): 1–42.

Moreland, W.H., ed., *Pieter Floris: His Voyage to the East Indies in the Globe, 1611–1615* (London: Hakluyt Society, 1934).

Morga, A. de, *Sucesos de las Islas Filipinas*, tr. and ed. J.S. Cummins (Cambridge: Cambridge University Press for the Hakluyt Society, 1971).

Muhammad Yusof Hashim, *The Malay Sultanate of Malacca*, tr. D.J. Muzaffar Tate (Kuala Lumpur: Dewan Bahasa dan Pustaka, 1992).

Pinto, P.J. de Sousa, *Portugueses e Malaios: Malaca e os Sultanatos de Johor e Achém, 1575–1619* (Lisbon: Sociedade Histórica da Independência de Portugal, 1997).

————, *The Portuguese and the Straits of Melaka, 1575–1619: Power, Trade and Diplomacy* (Singapore: NUS Press, 2012).

Pires, T., *The Suma Oriental of Tome Pires: An Account of the East from the Red Sea to Japan. Written in Malacca and India in 1512–1515*, ed. A. Cortesão, 2 vols. (London: Hakluyt Society, 1944).

Relação das Plantas & Descripções de todas as Fortalezas, Cidades & Povoações que os Portuguezes tem no Estado da India Oriental (Lisbon: Biblioteca Nacional, 1936).

Roff, W.R., *The Origins of Malay Nationalism* (Kuala Lumpur and Singapore: The University of Malaya Press, 1967).

Rotterdam, Maritiem Museum, Collectie Dr. W.A. Engelbrecht, WAE 900–10.

Rouffaer, G.P., "Was Malaka Emporium vóór 1400 A. D. genaamd Malajoer? En waar lag Woerawari, Ma-Hasin, Langka, Batoesawar?", *Bijdragen en Mededelingen van het Koninklijk Instituut voor Taal-, Land- und Volkenkunde* 77 (1921): 1–174 and 359–604.

Roux, P. le, B. Sellato and J. Ivanoff, eds., *Poids e mesures en Asie du Sud-Est—Weights and Measures in Southeast Asia*, 2 vols. (Paris: École française de l'Extrême-Orient and Institut de Recherche sur le Sud-Est Asiatique, 2004–08).

Shellabear, W.G., *Sejarah Melayu* [The Malay Annals], 9th ed. (Singapore: Malaya Publishing House, 1961).

Sopher, D.E., *The Sea Nomads, a Study Based on Literature of the Maritime Boat People of Southeast Asia* (Singapore: Lim Bian Han, 1965).

Subrahmanyam, S., "Manila, Melaka, Mylapore…: A Dominican Voyage through the Indies, ca. 1600", *Archipel* 57 (1999): 223–42.

Temple, R.C., ed., *The Travels of Peter Mundy in Europe and Asia, 1608–1667*, vol. III, Travels in England, India, China, etc. (London: Hakluyt Society, 1919).

VOC Glossarium. Verklaringen van Termen, verzamelt uit de Rijksgeschiedkundige Publicatiën die betrekking hebben op de Verenigde Oost-Indische Compagnie (The Hague: Instituut voor Nederlandse Geschiedenis, 2000).

Winius, G.D. and C.C. Chorba, "Literary Invasions in La vida de Jacques de Coutre: do they prejudice its value as an historic source?", in *A Carreira da Índia e as Rotas dos Estreitos. Actas do VIII Seminário Internacional de História Indo-Portuguesa*, ed. A.T. de Matos and L.F.R. Thomaz (Angra do Heroísmo: Barbosa & Javier, 1998), pp. 709–19.

Wolters, O.W., *Early Indonesian Commerce: A Study of the Origins of Srivijaya* (Ithaca: Cornell University Press, 1967).

Yule, H. and A.C. Burnell, *Hobson-Jobson: A Glossary of Colloquial Anglo-Indian Words and Phrases*, reprint (Sittingbourne: Linguasia, 1994).

Web and Media Links

Bjaaland, P., review of *The Memoirs and Memorials of Jacques de Coutre*, 30 January 2014. http://www.goodreads.com/review/show/833834229

Goh, C., "Tales from the East. The Memoirs and Memorials of Jacques de Coutre", *The Star* (Kuala Lumpur), 10 June 2014, p. 15.

Gómez Rivas, L., "Quinientos años del descubrimiento del Pacífico", 29 January 2014. http://www.juandemariana.org/comentario/6474/quinientos/anos/descubrimiento/pacifico.

Morales, J.J., review of "The Memoirs and Memorials of Jacques de Coutre", *Asian Review of Book*, 26 January 2014. http://www.asianreviewofbooks.com/new/?ID=1732.

Zakir Hussain, "Rare look into South-East Asia from 400 Years Ago: Review of 'The Memoirs and Memorials of Jacques de Coutre'", *The Straits Times,* 18 January 2014, D17.